CONFESSIONS

OF A HIGH OFFICIAL

by Terumasa Mouri

As told to and translated

by Malcolm Hart

IN MEMORY

OF TERENCE DONOVAN

AND

TAMIYA JIRO

INTRODUCTION

When I wrote this story I had a movie in mind. Not a word story, a movie. I set about outlining this strange tale taking form in my mind.

In the movie trade, the would-be producer inevitably wants to know what the movie's about so you write an outline. He's expecting a couple of paragraphs. I gave him seventy pages. The movie had become a story

I picked it up, from a man in a bar Up Town New York… a seaman, from Nagasaki. He told me a strange, story. Opium. Golden Triangle. Viet Nam. Reincarnation. The President. Friends. Power. Corruption in high places. It was a good, Kiplingesque, kind of yarn. There was an historic truth in there, somewhere…

1.

I was at odds with the social order of things I was born into; from the very beginning I felt I'd entered this world at the wrong time. Modern life didn't suit me. I tried my best but even to this day I'm conscious of a distance between myself and the life going on around me, a sense of detachment, of not belonging.

I am a Terumasa and, at the time of this writing, the last in line of an old and some would say illustrious family. The Terumasa were Samurai, a sea-faring clan from Nagasaki serving Shoguns and Emperors for hundreds of years. When I was a child my grandfather regaled me with stories of our glorious past, stories of bravery, undying fidelity and honour. There was an elegance about Bushido, the traditional way of the warrior, that appealed to my innermost being but which I found sadly absent in modern life.

Nagasaki had been our home since it was little more than a fishing village. Over the years we'd accumulated some land, the ancestral castle at Sakuradai, a few small holdings that over the years grew in value. We were never ambitious for wealth and were trusted above most other families on account of it. Right up to the end of the Second World War we still enjoyed a position of trust with the Emperor. My father had commanded the Home Fleet as his father and his father's father had done before him; guarded the Emperor's door as it were.

My father did not share my sense of history. He was a man of his time, a modern Admiral commanding a modern fleet. He was still sensible of responsibility to Emperor and ancestors but in his life as a warrior traditional values seemed no longer to have meaning for him. They were colours of the past to be observed at ceremonies, not the code of honourable conduct they truly represented. Confidence to command was in his blood. On a ship or in the family he would brook no disobedience. We never were friends.

In 1940 I was twenty-six years old, a lieutenant of signals serving with a thousand other souls aboard the Hokusai, one of the Imperial Navy's new aircraft carriers. I had no enthusiasm for modern war and less for the way it was conducted. The navy unnerved me, lost as I was in its mindless numbers and calculations. I didn't belong. My father knew it. My reluctance to be what he and family tradition demanded of me angered him. I was an embarrassment, probably the biggest disappointment of his life.

I recall the last time we were all together as a family he was making a speech praising my young brother Kido's success and how proud he was of him. Turning to me unsmiling, he said my brother's dedication of spirit shamed me. I bowed my head in well-practiced humiliation. I couldn't have cared less about dedication of spirit but nevertheless genuinely happy Kido's life was working out well for him. We had always respected each other's differences. I was proud of him and he knew that.

My mother was a gentle woman in every sense. In an Edo style socially suitable marriage to my father she fulfilled the traditional role of wife to an important man with grace and forbearance. She made no show of emotion. If something pleased her a smile might creep to the corners of her mouth, if something displeased her she might frown a little. Kido and I didn't know her very well; being at school we were seldom alone with her but there was never any doubting her affection.

Fellow officers on the Hokusai found life straight

forward. The Admiral was Admiral, the Emperor was god and everything else fell tidily into place no one questioning a thing. There was no space in their lives for thinking. It was discouraged. Do what you're told! Do your duty! Enough of this thinking!

It's true some people sail through life without giving it a thought. Take Kido for example; we grew up together best of friends. Temperamentally we were quite different, almost opposites, but there was a love and respect between us that only brothers can know and it remains with me. He was kind and generous, well balanced and reliable but not a thinker at all and did very well for himself. By 1940 while I was languishing on the Hokusai he already had his own command, a minesweeper, a frigate of some kind. The navy wasn't a temporary commitment for either of us. It wasn't a contract that would one day end, it was our inevitable history. There was no avoiding it and we were expected to do our unthinking duty to the end.

Being the son of an admiral didn't make for an easy life in the navy. It created an attitude towards me both in my superiors and underlings I could not avoid. The officers I messed with on the Hokusai were all youngsters just out of Naval Academy. They were a modern generation with their jazz music and glossy magazines. We had little in common. They would play juvenile pranks to get my attention and I'd ignore them.

If any of them had any idea what I thought of them or the navy it wasn't from anything I ever said. I'd learned to be circumspect. But contempt has little need of word or gesture. I wasn't popular. "Unfriendly! No esprit de corps!", they accused me to my face. They were right of course. I wouldn't deny it.

Suddenly my life was blown onto a completely different tack. That summer of 1940 the Hokusai was engaged in fleet exercises. We were a few days out and the ward room nonsense was already beginning to test my patience when out of the blue came an order transferring Lieutenant Terumasa off that floating tin shithouse and its tedious company back to base immediately! I might have thought it was a joke, the youngsters playing one of their games but there was no question of it. I was on duty; I took the message myself. I remember the euphoria, the feeling of relief.

I'd no idea what I was in for. Reprimand? Promotion? I didn't care. It was the only thing that ever happened to me in the navy everyone was happy about. They were really pleased to see me go. They couldn't have been more friendly. They drank my health and dropped me off a few days later in Yokohama. In Yokohama all the Base Commander could tell me was I had to report immediately to my father in Tokyo.

My heart sank. The mind struggled to make sense of it as I boarded the train. It's unusual for an individual, a non-entity, to be withdrawn from a battle group on exercise at such short notice. Why would my father do that? What was his hurry? Had there been a death in the family? My mother? Why else would he even want to see me? I was the bane of his life. The mind wandered on as the train sped towards Tokyo.

2

He welcomed me briefly, unable to refrain from immediately firing the same old salvos at me, my lack of progress compared with how well Kido was doing. Then he'd go on about loyalty, duty to the Emperor, the family and all that. I was patient, I was used to it. I'd let him say his piece and mumble the appropriate apologies and promises.

Then silence. He frowned while gathering his thoughts. I waited. Shaking his head as though he still could not believe what he was about to tell me, he said the Baron Kawakami had personally requested my services.

I was as surprised as he was. I looked up expecting to know why but that was the beginning and end of it. He had no idea what it was about and couldn't imagine what the Baron could possibly want with someone of my uncertain temperament. Whatever the Baron had in mind, my father expected me to be a credit to the Terumasa. That's all that mattered to him.

As I was leaving he slipped for a moment from 'Admiral' to 'Father'. He even smiled. He thought, perhaps, in the elevated circles of society in which the Baron undoubtedly moved I'd find myself a suitable wife. My brother, after all, was married and already had two children. And then, the Admiral again, he advised I wouldn't get anywhere in the world if I didn't show myself to be as other men. I bowed myself out.

That the Baron Kawakami had never married, yet was one of the most powerful men in Japan, seemed to have evaded my father's notice. In truth he knew little about anything that wasn't to do with the navy. A chauffeur-driven car was waiting to take me to the Baron's castle some thirty kilometres to the north of the city.

Like my father, I couldn't imagine what Kawakami could want of me. He hardly knew me. The Terumasa and Kawakami were related through my mother by marriage. He would call me nephew because it suited the discrepancy in our age but I was more likely a cousin three or four times removed. As I am now, he was then all that remained of one of Japan's oldest dynasties, last in line and childless.

He was a leading architect of change in Japan, largely responsible for our industrialisation and entry into free trade with the rest of the world. As manufacturers we were second to none but the need to import all the raw materials for our industries left us vulnerable. We depended on the British colonies for their rubber, coal, and tin and on the Dutch for oil. Our relationship with them was delicate. They were uncomfortable with our progress, competing as we were in markets that had been for so long their own province. They could turn us on or off like a tap if they so wished.

Most of our international relationships at that time were under stress. We'd been at war with Russia for as long as anyone could remember and had been committed to aggressive military action in Manchuria since 1931. In our metamorphosis from mediaeval to modern, political parties had emerged with a distinct military bent and the army was beginning to influence and shape our foreign policy.

The Baron had gained more than anyone from the changes he'd helped bring about. He owned seventy per cent of Japan's steel production and manufactured anything that could be made from it. Ships, aeroplanes, cars, cameras, armaments, electronics, cans, pots and pans, cigarette lighters, toys, anything you can think of. He was as wealthy as the Emperor.

3.

It was early evening when I arrived at his castle, a classical Edo mansion. Beyond, the distant snow-cap of Fujiyama gleamed in the last rays of the setting sun. I was met at the door by an elderly matron.

His household was run entirely by women. Three beautiful young women in kimono and obi took my hat, coat and valise and brought me to the room prepared for me while another prepared my toilet. I bathed and dressed in a linen kimono bearing the arms of the house of Kawakami. I felt a tingle of apprehension as I did at school when summoned by a master. One of the young women led me upstairs to meet my cousin.

The room was softly lighted. The Baron was sitting in a European armchair, his right leg resting on an upholstered stool, an ebony walking stick leaned against the chair.

He looked like a Buddha, at least eighty years old, bald and slightly over weight. As I entered, his old lined face, cigarette stuck in the middle, creased into a broad grin. He lowered his eyelids in response to my low and respectful bow. Calling me nephew, he said how kind it was of me to arrive at such short notice and how sorry he was for the haste. He waved me to a chair. His female retainers fussed around him brushing ash from his lap, refilling his cup with sake.

The young women fluttered around me, poured sake, offered me the Baron's oval English cigarettes. I don't smoke. I never have. They were charming.   Then he shouted for them to get out and leave us alone. He took a good-humoured swipe at one of them with his ebony stick and they all fled giggling. The Baron was old but it was clear his fire still burned brightly.

We sat in silence sipping and refilling cups of sake. The cigarette burned on in the middle of his face, ash fell into his lap unheeded. I watched as he lit another. I could see the smoking was going to be a problem. He smiled a lot, smiled as he spoke relishing every syllable. For a man his age he had a firm, untrembling voice.

"We live in dangerous times, nephew, times of extraordinary upheaval in the world. Danger is all around us. It is dangerous to move, perhaps even more dangerous to stand still."

He talked like a poet.

"If we are to survive as a modern, industrial nation we have to dance nimbly and be prepared to take risks."

He only removed the cigarette from his lips occasionally to sip his sake. He tapped his cradled leg with his stick.

"I'm an old man with old legs. You are going to be my

young legs, Terumasa Mouri, young legs I can trust."

I nodded of course without having the least idea what he meant. Legs he can trust? A messenger boy? An equerry perhaps? Not such a bad job. Or did he mean an apprentice, an associate groomed to take over? He was very old after all. He had no heirs. The thought occurred to me. You know how the mind runs on.

Then he ordered me to have no further contact with family or friends. He was emphatic. I was now on active service bound by the highest order of secrecy.

"You are Samurai, nephew. You understand such things."

Honoured by this recognition but still mystified, I nodded. He went on.

"We leave tomorrow morning for the United States of America, Washington, to meet an old friend who thinks he might have the solution to some of our problems."

He inclined his head inviting questions.

I had nothing to say.

He clapped his hands, all smiles again. Two of the

young women came in to brush the ash from his lap and put him to bed. He wished me a good night.

In the chamber allotted to me I lay down to sleep, his words turning over in my mind. A friend in America who could solve our problems? Problems? What problems? We were to dance nimbly? Be prepared to take risks? What on earth did he mean?

4.

In the Rolls Royce the Baron smoked incessantly all the way to his private airport. On the runway, sleek and silver, gleaming and trembling in the early morning sunlight, stood the latest in aeronautical design from Mitsubishi, its twin engines ticking over. Getting out of the car, I politely offered Kawakami my hand and he rapped my knuckles with his stick. I bowed. It was going to be a long trip. The Baron limping on his stick, we walked slowly to the aeroplane.

Designed as a medium range bomber, it had been customised to suit the Baron's needs. The body of the aircraft was sealed and air conditioned. There were state rooms for the Baron and myself and an area between furnished as a conference room, a table with chairs either side. Quarters for stewards and a chef were at the rear of the plane. Even by today's standards it was very comfortable. As soon as we were aboard he dragged me around inspecting every detail, proudly showing off the plane's cunning mechanical innovations. It had been built by one of his own companies.

We sat in silence in the conference room waiting for take off. The Baron smoked. The plane jolted into motion and we were away. The problems Kawakami was going to discuss with his friend in Washington were obviously of sufficient importance for him to travel half way around the world to meet with him. I was curious of course, curious without realising I was being drawn into the mysteries of a reality quite different from the mundane life I had been leading. To me, at that time, it was simply an assignment, another job. I had no idea.

Kawakami spent the daytime in his state room emerging only at sunset. I spent most of the trip on my bunk reading. He'd given me a quantity of papers and pamphlets, most of them on Asian affairs. He required me to join him every evening in the conference room for dinner and discussion.

We'd eat, drink cup after cup of sake, he'd smoke and we'd talk long into the night.

He dreamed of a Greater Asian Society. There'd been talk of it in political circles. He grew excited. He had great plans. He was looking at South East Asia, the tin, the rubber, the oil our industries so desperately needed, so essential to our security and prosperity. After backing the highly successful Manchurian Railway adventure he was now on good terms with the army and with Tojo, his best customer for armaments.

War had already broken out in Europe and we had signed a non-aggression pact with Hitler who was already trashing the colonial powers. Holland had fallen, France almost. It was only a matter of time before they and the British went under. He said with Tojo and the army behind him the time was ripe. We could take whatever we liked from the beleaguered westerners, their colonies were poorly defended. He made it sound so easy.

His credibility vacillated in my confused mind. Sometimes I thought he was crazy, sometimes convinced he was a genius. There is a kind of holy madness about those driven by the pursuit of power. But his ideas were plausible and any fool could see a military build-up was underway.

He said the moment we'd concluded the non-aggression pact with Hitler and Mussolini, our Chiefs of Staff had started fantasising about a conquest of South East Asia, Burma, India and a meeting of victorious German and Japanese armies somewhere around Egypt. He chuckled and poured more sake. He was dealing with matters of great magnitude, ideas greater than anything he had ever entertained before. He was cresting his wave. I shuddered at the thought of its enormity. It wasn't until we were nearing the end of our journey, we were flying across America when he revealed the precise nature of the problem we were coming to Washington to solve.

America. His expansionist ideas wouldn't work if we had to fight America. Once aroused, even Tojo agreed, she'd be far too powerful an enemy to be met headlong. South East Asia would be easy but war against America would be suicide. So that was the problem. To take what we needed from South East Asia without America becoming involved. His friend in Washington had been working on it.

We landed in Washington DC after nearly two weeks of island-hopping across thousands of miles of Pacific Ocean and the entire American continent, crossing date lines and time zones, only touching down to refuel. It was the middle of the night when we arrived. I had no idea what night or what time it was. I'd been sick for the last twenty four hours, suffocating on the Baron's incessant smoking. It penetrated the air conditioning and stank up the whole plane. It was impossible to get away from. I didn't care where I was as long as there was fresh air.

Our Ambassador was there to meet us and drive us back to the embassy in Georgetown. He used his own latch key to let us in, he'd sent the staff to bed. He ushered us into an elegant nineteenth century drawing room, the clock on the mantelpiece struck one. He offered us tea but the Baron declined telling him to await the arrival of our expected guest then take himself off to bed.

Kawakami smoked while we waited. For an old man he maintained his energy well. I was exhausted and having difficulty staying awake. The door bell rang shortly after three o'clock. It startled me and I jumped to my feet. The Baron waved me back to my chair. The drawing room door opened, a man came in, the door closed silently behind him. He was tall and lightly built, a European in a baggy linen suit.

My first impression was hazy, I couldn't be sure of his age. His hair was thinning but in that light I couldn't tell if it was fair or grey. He could have been seventy but the way he walked, light as a dancer, suggested he was much younger. His skin too, his face and hands, everything about him was taught and youthful, everything but his eyes. They were icy blue like a Malamute and as old as God. He was a smiler like the Baron. They were smiling at each other.

"Good evening, Harpur..."

The Baron waved his cigarette in my direction.

"My nephew, Terumasa Mouri."

The icy eyes were on me. His voice was soft, every syllable distinct. He spoke perfect Japanese.

"Good evening. The Baron speaks highly of you."

I got to my feet, bowing. Ignoring me, he walked across to Kawakami and sat down next to him. This is exactly what he said.

"The President congratulates you on the conclusion of

your agreement with Herr Hitler and Signor Mussolini and now he's ready to move. He proposes an attack on one of his possessions. Oahu, Pearl Harbor, perhaps, would provide a suitable debut. Towards the end of next year? He'd like your views."

I had the sensation the room was drifting away, receding. The hand at the end of my sleeve looked small and distant as though it no longer belonged to me. My palms were sweating and somewhere between my ears a buzzing. I shook myself. The Baron glanced at me reprovingly as he lit another cigarette. Harpur stood and glided towards the door. He looked across at the Baron.

"One last thing Kawakami. The President thinks there's no profit for you in either India or Burma."

He looked at me, then at the Baron again.

"...but otherwise, take what you can get."

The Baron smiled and said everything was to his satisfaction. India? Burma? Fine. He'd return to Tokyo immediately and get things started. Another brief exchange of smiles and Harpur was gone.

The Baron struggled to his feet, grinning from ear to ear,

clapping his hands, unable to contain his delight. Wheezing and coughing and brushing deserts of ash from his frock coat he lit another cigarette. He was very pleased with himself. We had a plane to catch.

My head was spinning. Who the hell was Mister Harpur? What was his authority? What was the meaning of this meeting? Kawakami had said his friend had a solution to Japan's perceived problems. I'd thought perhaps this friend would offer ways and means to sort things out through diplomatic channels but that was not the case. His plan in order to allow Japan to wage war in the Pacific undisturbed required us to first attack the United States. What kind of madness was that? He and Kawakami had obviously considered it and discussed it long before this meeting. This Mister Harpur, whoever he was, had the confidence of the President who had obviously ratified his plan.

5.

I know what you're thinking. You're saying to yourself old Mouri's crazy! He can't expect me to believe that! That's not the way things happen! That's not the way it was! The President a cold and calculating devil? The fate of the world decided by strange men in baggy linen suits that come in out of the night? Aged nicotine addicts? I would never have believed it myself if I hadn't been there, heard with my own ears, seen with my own eyes.

This extraordinary experience catapulted me into a new reality. The world as I had previously perceived it was a fairy tale. Behind the romance lurked sinister and manipulative powers. The President and Kawakami were power seekers. Whether in their own interest or in the interest of the nation they lead made little difference, they scurried feverishly around like gold-seeking prospectors looking for ways to increase their personal power. They were certainly not working for the greater good of humanity,

In those days Europe was the centre of world power. It had been so for over five hundred years. After the first World War it began coming apart at the seams and now, with the Nazis and Fascists running amuck, everything was up for grabs. It wasn't to do with human rights, democracy or any other social nicety, Hitler and Mussolini were fighting to take over the power, world power, from dynasties grown too decadent and corrupt, too feeble to defend themselves.

In America, the President considered himself a likely contender but was being forced to sit on his side of the Atlantic and watch them having a free hand. Every time he pleaded with Congress to take an interest, to at least come to the aid of their friends in Europe, he got the same response. They didn't want any part of it. Their mandate from the American people was for peace, isolation, avoidance. They were for minding their own business. They had troubles of their own.

The President wasn't motivated by sentiment. Maybe he was disturbed at the plight of his English speaking friends but his real concern was that Herr Hitler, uncontested, would take over the reins of world power. He was looking for a way to get involved and needed an excuse, a reason that would convince Congress it was in the best interest of the American people. He was looking for an excuse to brawl with the Nazis and we were going to give him one.

That was Harpur's plan. Now we were Hitler's allies, our enemies would become Hitler's enemies. We would attack an American possession and bring them into the war. In return the President would guarantee us a free hand in the Pacific and South East Asia.

On the way home we had clearance through Honolulu. As our plane banked and headed out to sea, we passed directly over the United States Naval Base at Pearl Harbor. It was a fine summer morning. Battleships of all classes lazed at their moorings, wisps of smoke at the top of their stacks. Trucks crawled up and down wharves. I could see tiny figures of men getting their day under way. I identified some of the ships. It was a very old fleet, so old it push came to shove it would even have had trouble with our navy. I could see why the President wasn't worried about us bombing it, we'd be doing him a favour.

The Baron took photographs through the cabin portholes as long as the harbour was in view. His hands trembled so violently with excitement I doubt the pictures were ever of use to anyone.

6.

It took Kawakami no time at all to sell the stratagem to the Imperial High Command but he and I remained the only ones who knew all the nuances and ramifications. Generals didn't have to know the whys and wherefores, they couldn't have cared less anyway. Ever since their easy victories in Manchuria they'd been chafing at the bit, anxious to demonstrate their skill and courage again. They were Tojo's boys! They'd take on anybody! They weren't great thinkers. America? No problem! No one was too big for them. Japan and Germany would rule the world between them! The Baron didn't have to sell them the plan, it was all he could do to hold them back.

The navy wasn't entirely convinced. They didn't get swept up in the generals' enthusiasm until Kawakami suggested our first objective might be the American fleet at anchor in Pearl Harbor. They immediately saw the strategic logic of this, became fascinated by the impossibility of the task, almost obsessive, a personal challenge you could say. Kawakami encouraged them. The High Command commissioned Admiral Yamamoto to work out a plan. The rest is history.

I've never been a gambling man but the Sunday of the attack on Pearl Harbor was like going to the race track for the first time, drawn into the thrill of win or lose. I began to experience the sensation of power, a sensation so pleasurable to Kawakami that he invested all his waking hours in its pursuit. He was perfectly calm right up to the day. Then, that Sunday morning, he was so keyed up I thought he would have a heart attack. God! How he smoked!

I'll never forget it. Even the Baron's smoking didn't bother me as we sat, excited as children, waiting for news, developments, reports of reactions from around the world. We'd detonated a volcano and lava was about to belch out all over the place. Would we be engulfed? Would there be treachery? Would the President respond as he'd promised? It was too late to worry. The chips were down, the race was on.

I have to admit I was shocked by the ferocity of America's reaction. The news media, in no time at all, had that apathetic, isolationist, new-deal nation on its feet, all differences dismissed, a snarling monster war machine impatient to kill. I'd never imagined such a sudden change about possible. I feared the worst.

Kawakami on the other hand was in some kind of ecstasy as the dreadful flower of his genius slowly blossomed before us, everything going according to plan. We bombed Pearl Harbor, the President declared war on us and our allies. He convinced Congress, now they were at war with Hitler, that Europe was the primary theatre. The American army was sent across the Atlantic and we were left alone in the Pacific as he'd promised. We could do more or less as we pleased.

If you're my age you'll remember the events. If you're too young you'll find they've been well documented and entered into history. The way our armies swept victorious, virtually uncontested, through colonial South East Asia and the Pacific. In a few months we'd conquered as far west as Thailand, taken the Philippines and every island in the Pacific Basin as far south as New Guinea. We had everything we needed. It looked as though Kawakami had pulled it off.

I accompanied him to a number of victory parties in Tokyo, drunken meetings of the Joint Chiefs of Staff, the same bunch at every party. There were always one or two politicians around, one or two ministers perhaps, but by and large they were military gatherings. As an unimportant aide I watched from the back as they toasted each other's victories. They were very pleased with themselves. They had no idea.

It was bound to happen. At one party, five or six of them cornered the Baron seeking his support for a plan to take advantage of the situation and pursue the fleeing enemy through Burma and India. I remembered Harpur's words and looked across at Kawakami. I caught his eye but he looked away. He listened with polite interest as Generals and Admirals drunkenly resurrected their favourite fantasy, to meet up with the Germans in Egypt. Kawakami was non-committal. He promised them he'd give it his consideration. I could tell he was getting excited again.

It was about one in the morning when we got back to the castle. For the first time I can remember, Kawakami asked me to help him from the car. He was trembling. I gave him my hand and he wouldn't let go of it. He steered me into the house and instead of letting me go to bed, tightened his grip. He steered me slowly into his library. A servant followed us in to switch on the lights but he waved her away, slumped into his armchair and lit a cigarette. We sat in silence in the darkened room. He smoked. I waited. He started talking, not to me but to himself. He made a face as if there was a bad taste in his mouth.

"They treat us like dogs. They've treated us like dogs from the very beginning, ever since they arrived on our shores. They want us to trade with them, buy their garbage, but they don't want us to get too rich. The power's not for us! They want us to be the paupers of their miserable society! They think they own the whole fucking world!"

Saliva had extinguished the cigarette between his lips. His eyes roamed the ceiling as if searching the shadows for something. Then he closed them, smiling. He hummed a little tune. I could tell he was working up to something.

"We're at the cross-roads, nephew. It's now or never. We'll fuck them once and for all while they're squabbling like jackals over the carcass of Europe. Why not?"

I shuddered. He was going over the top. He opened his eyes, smiling.

"You know, nephew, we've many friends in India and Burma."

Friends? What the hell had friends got to do with it? What about Harpur! I started having dreams that night, disturbing dreams of snarling dog deities with cold blue eyes; bloody saliva dripped from their maws, razor-sharp teeth snapped. The mind was working overtime.

7.

Gambling on the Americans having their hands full in Europe and North Africa, Kawakami made his last play. He staked everything, not just his own wealth, he put the whole nation on the line, Emperor, everything.

Our army skipped across Thailand and cut quickly through southern Burma. Thailand was neutral and we made a deal with them for free passage of our troops. At the gates of India the army turned north into the mountains and jungles of the central Burmese plateau. It was then the Baron received a terse message from Harpur, the first communication we'd had with him since our meeting in Washington.

I suppose Kawakami expected some kind of protest from him, some rebuke for disregarding their agreement, but he couldn't have cared less. He was going for broke. The old fool was heading for Egypt.

There were two things that interested me about the message other than the message itself. One, the unusual way it had been routed to us, delivered by hand to our consulate in Bern, Switzerland by a Swiss national, a member of the Theosophical Society. The other thing of astonishing interest to me was its place of origin. Harpur lived in Lashio.

Lashio? I'd never heard of it. I looked it up on the map and after much searching finally found it. A small town in the northernmost Shan State of Burma nestled between Tibet, Thailand and China, one of the most remote places on earth. I was flabbergasted. I'd always assumed Harpur lived in America. I couldn't believe it! He'd warned us! He lived in Burma and we'd brought our war to his doorstep.

When I told Kawakami he treated the whole thing very lightly. He was an old gambler at the far end of his life. He didn't care. What did he have to lose? Things looked very different from where I sat. My cousin had been mistaken. The odds were more heavily stacked against us than he'd realised.

Our bewildered Generals began suffering unaccustomed reverses in the field. Suddenly it seemed the Pacific was full of American warships. Hundreds of thousands of American soldiers spilled out onto the beaches of our short-lived empire. We suffered one ignominious defeat after another. Within a year they'd thrown a noose around us and were drawing it tight.

The Baron barely lived to regret his indiscretion. During the first bombing of Tokyo, he passed quietly away, leaving us to answer for his worldly misdeeds. His last cigarette fell from his dead lips into the bedding. He actually cremated himself. Took the whole castle with him.

8.

Tokyo was in chaos. Communications had completely broken down. The centre of the city had been badly bombed, the wood and paper neighbourhoods around the city devastated by magnesium incendiaries and the ashes blown to dust by high explosives. The hardest of men would have found it difficult to deal with such human suffering, such misery.

After Kawakami's official cremation I tried to reconnect with my family. All transport out of the city had been suspended and there was no telephone communication with Nagasaki. I walked to the Admiralty thinking I might find my father there, any port in a storm. He wasn't there but I bumped into an elderly colleague of his, a desk sailor who brought me up to date.

My father had been in Yokohama two days ago to refuel and had sailed right out again. He'd been at sea for the past two months fighting a brilliant rear guard action and they were awaiting word on his position. They'd heard nothing from him for thirty-six hours. He was probably maintaining radio silence. You know how it is.

I knew how it was. It didn't sound promising. I asked if there was any news of my brother. The old man was embarrassed. Didn't I know? Hadn't I heard? My brother'd been listed missing in action for over a month. Went down off Okinawa, all hands. The old man was sincerely moved, sympathetic. He'd known my brother and I all our lives.

Suddenly I felt the weight upon me. What was happening? What the hell was going on? Why wasn't anyone doing anything to stop it getting worse? I hadn't eaten for days and felt nauseous. The old man said I didn't look well, I should sit down. He was a good friend. He closed the door of his office. As soon as I was breathing easier I asked him straight out. What was happening? What was the true state of affairs?

He was happy to tell me everything he knew. The army was preparing to fight to the last man, woman and child rather than surrender. What else could you expect? Things were pretty bad. He went to the door, opened it, looked out into the corridor and closed it again. The Emperor had backed an initiative to end the war on terms sympathetic to our national and spiritual character. He'd sent emissaries to the neutral governments of Sweden, Switzerland and the Soviets seeking their intercession. Only one of them had responded, only the Russians. It was old Naotake Satō, our ambassador. They kept him waiting in the Kremlin two weeks, and today, this very morning, he'd been invited to meet with their Foreign Secretary who'd promptly handed him a declaration of war. Can you beat that?

No. I couldn't beat it. I was sure this was the end. I said goodbye to the old fellow and walked out into the humid hazy August afternoon. I don't know where I went, I just walked. It was all getting too much for me. My Samurai soul was being torn apart. My mind was confused, I didn't know what to think or do. My mother, my family far away in Nagasaki, my father and brother dead. Revenge burned in my heart, anger clouded my vision. One moment I was ready to race off to Nagasaki and the next I was in a state of patriotic fervour looking for a ship, a regiment to join. I didn't know if I was coming or going. An air-raid siren brought me to my senses. Self-preservation overrides every emotion. I took shelter in the basement of a department store.

It was in that basement, huddled together with hundreds of frightened people I didn't even know, young and old, men, women and children, bombs exploding on the streets and buildings above us, it was during that raid I suddenly saw my duty, saw what I had to do clear as day.

I had to get to Harpur. In my confusion I seemed to have a clear idea he was the only person living who could do anything about the state of affairs, the only person who could put a stop to all this insanity. I was crazy.

9.

It's surprising how easy it is at times like that, a society in disarray, restraints crumbling yet still vaguely coherent, you can get away with anything if you have the confidence. I had the confidence of the insane. Samurai zeal burned in my breast.

Getting a plane was easy, easier than getting the fuel for it. There was a lot of haphazard traffic between military bases and, in the turmoil, it wasn't that difficult to get around, it just required determination of which I had plenty, a warrior on a mission to save his Emperor from further ignominy. As I flew long hours into the night, night after night for at least a week, my tired mind reflected on the irony, the historical stance of the Terumasa, the Emperor's strong right arm. We hopped from one safe haven to the next, hoping to escape detection, hoping we'd be able to land, hoping we'd be able to take off again, always scavenging for food and gasoline.

On an airfield in Thailand I met a sympathetic pilot. We were both having tea in the officers' mess. I was looking for a lift to take me closer to my final destination. He said, if it was any help to me, he was flying medical supplies and ammunition up to Rangoon; I was welcome to come along.

We had a few hours to kill. We chatted. I told him I had to get to Lashio on diplomatic business; I showed him my papers. Of course I didn't mention Harpur, he'd have thought I was a loony. He said if there were no orders waiting for him in Rangoon he'd fly me up there. I warmed to him thinking perhaps he was as crazy as I was.

His plane was one of Kawakami's Mitsubishis but stripped for war. Two pilots and a navigator/radio operator. Shivering in civilian clothes I huddled with them in the cockpit, the warmest place in the plane. As we crossed the Burmese coastline we got buffeted by all kinds of flack from the sea. We had no intelligence, didn't know who was who; radio silence; no lights. It could have been anybody, possibly one of our own. Anyway, we got hit by a shell exploding off our starboard wing. The starboard engine took a bit of shrapnel and started to smoke and splutter. That's all we needed. If the plane caught fire we'd go off like a firework. We didn't have far to go and as we lost altitude the rain extinguished the smouldering fire. We limped into Rangoon just as dawn was breaking. I remember it as if it was yesterday, the sun rising through shredded storm clouds giving us the impression the worst was over and a new day was beginning.

The navigator switched on the radio to make contact with the tower but couldn't get through. The wavelength was jammed with a message repeated over and over. That's what it sounded like, a message, great chunks of it blotted out by atmospherics and static. We couldn't make sense of it. Bombing; armed forces; extraordinary circumstances; surrender? As we crawled out of the aircraft, the message, that's what it was, was being broadcast on the airfield's PA system. It was the Emperor speaking to the nation, asking us to bear the unbearable. He told us of the bombing of Hiroshima and Nagasaki. He told us we'd surrendered.

Despair hung like fog over that airfield. I wandered around aimlessly. Aircraft were scattered all over the place in a state of suspended animation. Engine cowlings open, gas lines and belts of bullets trailed from wings and fuselages, groups of ground crew huddled beneath them getting drunk. Here and there, men waved swords and pistols, ranting and raving, young officers my own age, some younger. A bullet in the head. A way out of the shame and humiliation. The way of the warrior.

I stumbled into the administration building, into the adjutant's office. A veteran sergeant sat at the desk, a half empty bottle of whisky to the side. He was going through papers and documents as if nothing had happened, initialling, stamping, nothing it seemed could disturb him. He glanced up at me as I entered then returned his attention to his papers as if they were all that mattered in the world. His business-as-usual attitude brought me to my senses. I asked him where was the Commanding Officer. He replied without even looking up.

"Dead, sir."

The adjutant? Where was the adjutant?

"Dead, sir."

He jabbed his thumb at the door behind him, calm as anything. I walked past him into the inner office. They'd both shot themselves by the look of it. I was numb. What were another two bodies?

I asked the sergeant if there'd been any news from Nagasaki.

"Nothing on the radio since yesterday."

Concerned for my family I asked if there'd been many casualties. He paused from his work. Gave me an odd look.

"You haven't heard, then...?"

I shook my head. He whistled...

"It was an atom bomb..."

I'd never heard of such a thing.

"An atom bomb?"

He took a swig from the bottle of whisky.

"Seventy five thousand dead in an instant! The fellow on the radio said the explosion was like the light of ten thousand suns. The sky turned brown. Not a building left standing."

He took another swig from the bottle and returned his attention to his papers.

In that moment my mind went blank. there was nothing left for me. My whole family almost certainly dead, the nation surrendered? I couldn't figure out what on earth I was doing in this strange country? What was I doing on this insane airfield thousands of miles from home?

And then I remembered! That's right! I was on my way to Harpur! Where was my pilot? Suddenly I was back on course. I'd lost all memory of why I was actually trying to get to Harpur but whatever it was now seemed to be of burning importance. I strode out of the building yelling for my friend the pilot at the top of my voice.

Now there was purpose again. I needed purpose. Right then I needed purpose more than anything. I had to get to Harpur, it didn't matter why, it was just damned important.

He was the last piece on the board still standing.

10.

As I said, my pilot was no slouch and I had no difficulty finding him, in fact he was already looking for me. He'd promised to get me to Lashio. He'd deal with all the emotional stuff when he returned, there'd be time to sort it all out later. What a man! He'd found us a small, high-wing monoplane, the type used by artillery for spotting, economical on gas and could land and take off on a postage stamp. As soon as we'd left the ground he brought out food he'd scavenged at the airfield commissary. A feast. Rice and great slabs of smoked fish. We hadn't eaten in days and as we flew steadily north we stuffed our faces. He brought out a bottle of sake and we washed the food down.

I don't know how long I slept but when he woke me it was late afternoon. By his calculations we were there and we should keep our eyes peeled for an airstrip.

I looked down on rolling orange hills and blood-red rivers. He brought us down to about five hundred feet. Nothing. Absolutely nothing. He identified the Nam Yao river, there was even a single railway line but no landing strip, no town. He was sure of his navigation, he was sure it was our river. We followed it across a plain and at the far side, by now little more than a stream, it rose into the foothills of the Himalayas and there was Lashio, a cluster of buildings in the shadow of the hills and there was even a landing strip.

The food and sleep on the flight helped restore my spirits and made it possible for me to keep going. That was the point, to keep going, an end in itself. To shut down the mind's song and dance long enough, to shut out the pathetic scene on Rangoon airfield, the Emperor's speech, the seppuku. Harder still to shut out the atom bomb and the extinction of my family. Blown away like insects! Gone! Just like that.

Maybe I thought Harpur was to blame for all that hellish madness, my misfortunes, for everything. Maybe he was. Whatever, he became my focus. When I stepped down from the plane he was the focus of all the anger, bitterness, frustration and hate that had settled like demons in my craw. Only an act of Samurai vengeance could exorcise them.

The local people heard us coming. No doubt the arrival of an aeroplane was a singular event in their lives. They'd all turned out to watch us land. They sat, stood and squatted in silent groups at the end of the runway. We taxied up to them. They didn't move.

I asked my friendly pilot for his pistol. He gave it to me along with a package, the remains of the rice and smoked fish. I took one last pull at the sake bottle and waved him goodbye. He yelled he'd wait until I was safely on my way.

I had no idea of Harpur's exact location but it didn't bother me. I thought in that remote part of the world if one man knew everyone knew. I was right. I went through a number of possible pronunciations of Harpur's name until I finally hit on one that did the trick. Lots of tongue clicking and head nodding and, by the pained expression on their faces and massive gestures of their arms in the direction of the peaks behind them, I gathered Harpur lived a long way away, all the way to the neck of the valley.

Among my audience were two or three seedy-looking mules. I approached their owners. I took out a fistful of yen and pointed to the strongest looking animal. The owner looked me up and down, felt the material of my overcoat, studied my shoes. I made a deal. I got the mule of my choice in exchange for my overcoat, jacket, hat and shoes. I mounted up, pistol tucked in the waistband of my trousers, the food in my pocket, my necktie around my forehead. I waved to the pilot. He swung the plane around and opened the throttle. My discarded yen were caught by his slip stream and blown to the wind as he raced off down the runway.

11.

That night I practically froze to death. The mule saved me. I rode him for as long as I could, for as long as I had the strength to cling to his back. Then, as night fell, I looked for shelter. It was dark before I could find anything vaguely suitable and had to settle for the leeward side of a hillock. I tethered my faithful mule while I ate a little food to muster my strength, then I tied his legs and pushed him over. He struggled a bit but he was as exhausted as I was. I cuddled into his warm belly and we were both soon asleep.

The following day started badly. The mule woke me by pissing all over my legs. Worse, in the night I'd developed a raging fever. I felt like death. I ate a little rice and got back on the mule. What a sight we must have been! Ragged, dirty, unshaven. When we passed locals they looked at me strangely. I didn't care, I was barely conscious of anything. I hardly remember the journey at all. I've no idea how long it took, amazed I ever accomplished it, I was so sick, burning up with the fever. By the time I caught sight of Harpur's house I was so sick I thought I was hallucinating. We rounded a bend and there it was, high in the neck of the valley just above the timber line, shimmering in the sunlight. It looked like a palace or a monastery.

The valley below the house had been terraced and cultivated. The mule carried me slowly up the valley, terrace by terrace, both of us more dead than alive. I don't know how he did it but he got me there, right to the top, right to the gateway to the house. As I slipped from his back, both of us collapsed and he died. I struggled to my feet and staggered like a drunk, stumbling, falling, getting up, crawling.

Even in my feverish state I could not help but be

impressed by the house, its vast inward sloping stonewalls broken at higher levels by straight rows of windows and flat roofs. It was like a fortress.

Pistol drawn and cocked, I negotiated a narrow bridge that crossed a narrow ravine into the house itself. Burning with fever, soaked with sweat, I limped down corridors not knowing where I was, staggering into one empty room after another. There was no one, absolutely no one, no sign of life whatsoever, not a sound. I didn't know if I was awake or dreaming, alive or dead.

If you'd have asked me what I expected Harpur's house and household to be like, I couldn't have told you, I'd never given it a thought. I had no idea what to expect, I didn't know anything about him. It was strange enough he lived in such a god-forsaken corner of the world. So, when I tell you that the next door I stumbled through opened onto a large square room in which about a dozen men sat around the walls in silent meditation and that in their centre sat Harpur, well, that was about all I could take. I remember raising the pistol...

12.

It's easy to say now, but even then I had some sense of it, there was something inevitable, something providential about the way I got to Harpur's house. After all, it was no simple matter. Under those circumstances the odds must have been hundreds of thousands to one against. I'd only met the man once and if Kawakami had been straight with him and hadn't tried dealing from the bottom of the pack, who knows? I might never have set eyes on him again. But Kawakami cheated, brought all hell down on us and there I was.

I was the only person in the world who knew of his connection with Harpur. Their relationship had been very private. Power brokers operate very privately. They prefer no one to know of their existence let alone their Byzantine schemes, their plots and plans. As rich and powerful as he was, Kawakami wasn't a public figure, in Japan or anywhere else. Nor was Harpur. The limelight is for politicians, people who want to be king or president. Quite different kettles of fish. They adore pomp and ceremony, wanting to let the world know who's actually running things.

Kawakami and Harpur weren't like that. They avoided publicity. Fame held no attraction for them. And fortune?

They already had more than they could count. Their enjoyment lay in the thrill of being causal, of making things happen that otherwise wouldn't. Being God, you might say.

Anyway, I was suggesting there was something inevitable, preordained about my arrival at Harpur's house. I couldn't otherwise explain the feeling that I was expected.

***

When I awoke... it's all very hazy now... I seemed to surface several times before you could say I was clinically awake. A long shadowy journey back to consciousness, a mix of dreaming and waking, the waking like a dream. A room, a presence, the touch of cool fingers on my wrist then sleeping again to dream and wake again.

When I finally woke up I was in a room not unlike this, a simple room, a window with a view of mountains and deep blue sky. The air was warm, shadows of leaves played on the walls and ceiling. I was awake but had no strength to move. At first I just lay there, not even wondering where I was, I lay there feeling nothing, relaxed in the tranquillity. My eyes lazed amongst the leafy shadows, gazed out at snow-capped peaks and azure sky so pleasingly framed by the window.

But it didn't take long for the demons to return and for panic to set in. No time at all. Nor did I have the will to fight it. I just lay there and drove myself to distraction, recapitulating everything that had happened, the imagination dwelling greedily on the horror of it all. It wasn't until my body had regained some of its strength that I was able to control my over-active mind and start using it intelligently and give some constructive thought to my situation.

Twice a day, a man came into the room, a local fellow by his appearance, a local physician, maybe. He'd bring me food and take my pulse, sitting for as long as a half hour by my bedside each day, head bowed, fingers lightly on my wrist. He never uttered a word, not a sound. He came every day, twice a day until I was strong enough to get out of bed. Later, when I came to figuring out dates when things had happened, I didn't know it then but I'd been unconscious for a year.

During those days of recuperation I tried to give some kind of shape to my circumstances. Arriving the way I had, I had every reason to expect to be treated as a prisoner, a dangerous prisoner not to be trusted. After all, I'd tried to kill Harpur. Had I killed him? I didn't know. Whatever, I was sure there'd be a guard, someone to keep an eye on me. I thought about escape.

Escape? Where to? That long trek back to Lashio? The landing strip? What then? Where was I bound? Rangoon? Japan? What for? There was nothing for me in Japan, only the debris of a previous existence, memories and remains of a way of life I hadn't even been comfortable with. My mind stumbled along these lines as I crept out of bed for the first time. Hands trembling, I put on the clothes left for me, a pair of local-style cotton pants and a kind of shirt long to the knees.

Was I a prisoner? I edged painfully to the window and cautiously looked out. The house was cunningly built into the rock. The window was in an outside wall that fell precipitously away into the ravine. No way of escape there.

Escape? There's nothing to escape to!

What about the door? Is it locked? Try the door! I moved painfully back across the room to the door, slowly lifted the latch. Holding my breath, I opened it. Where's the guard? There was no guard. The corridor was empty.

It looked too easy. I made it to the end of the corridor. The place was deserted. Out into the warm sunshine. No one around. The small bridge and the open valley beyond. Nothing to stop me walking out.

Walk? Where to, you fool!

It took time for these stubborn reactive thoughts to simmer down. It was quite a while before I dropped the notion that I was a prisoner looking for a way of escape. Anyway, I was exhausted, I wanted to rest. The mountains soothed me. I felt removed from everything. It was easier to stay than to go.

13.

There were eleven others living at the house. I think there were eleven. Probably the only time I saw them together was when I burst in on them when I first arrived and in no mood to count them.

They were a strange and nameless company. They never

talked, not a word. One of them was the physician who'd cared for me and even he showed no sign of special recognition, didn't ask how I was feeling or anything like that. If they were communicating at all, they weren't doing it verbally.

It wasn't like a monastery or any kind of religious institution. There was no ritualised reverence, no rules, no uniforms. Everyone minded his own business, which suited me down to the ground. They were easy to live with. No posturing, no personality problems, no arguments. No one bumped into anyone else.

Mealtime was the nearest thing to a communal event. There was a big kitchen and one of them had obviously agreed to be the cook. His food wasn't very tasty but those wanting to eat it would congregate when it was ready and when it was eaten they'd leave again, disappearing back into the house somewhere. I learned very little about them. To this day I have no idea how they came to be there or what their relationship was to Harpur. Maybe each in turn had arrived to kill him, failed and decided to stay. Who knows? Anyway, as interesting as they may have been, their individual histories are not part of this story. I didn't get to know them in that way, their personal views, ambitions and so forth. Their particular importance to me, not something I understood at the time, was that they provided me with a background of basic sanity, a neutral tone against which events could be evaluated. As time passed, I found myself more and more in need of that kind of comparison.

Time was the first thing I had to deal with, getting from waking to sleeping without a program of things that had to be done. Until now my time had been accounted for by the multitude of petty, boring tasks imposed on me by modern life. There'd never been enough hours in a day, and none at all for things I genuinely enjoyed. I started constructing a formal garden, something I'd always wanted to do. At first it was mainly to occupy my surreptitious mind, ever ready at the drop of a hat to drag me back to the insanity of the past. Besides, I was a young man, I had a lot of energy, I needed the exercise. The garden absorbed the physical energy but I did it mainly to occupy the mind.

At school, in English class, I'd read with great interest the novel Robinson Crusoe. I'd been full of admiration for the way in which he had dealt with his adversity in isolation. Its recall aroused in me a sense of adventure. I turned my mind from the past and how it had brought me to this situation to a positive desire to make the best of things.

I realised with the onset of winter I would have to find warmer clothing. I set about a search of the house. The empty rooms were almost divest of furniture, There were dust marks on walls that suggested pictures or hangings had once adorned them, that some time in the past the house had been lived in by a more conventional family. In one room I found a travelling chest full of woollen blankets, some threadbare, some ravaged by the moth but enough of them in good enough order for me to fashion out of them layers of warm garments.

I found tools in a cupboard. They were old, rusted and falling apart, many of them too far gone for use, but there were enough, a pickaxe, a shovel, an axe, a saw and a twelve pound hammer that were retrievable. I spent the first winter at the house cleaning them up and by spring had them in mint condition, sharp and clean.

The garden I planned covered an acre and took that entire spring and all the following summer just to clear. I had in mind to start with a simple space open to the sky, a clear horizon. I'd almost done it but there was one rock left to move, a large one sticking up at an angle right in the middle. It was huge. It cluttered things up. It had to go.

I went at it with a fury day after day. Sometimes some of the silent ones would stand around watching me, amused. It was a chunk of granite half again the height of a man and five or six times his girth; the hammer just bounced off it. Nor could I get under it. There was no way of moving it so I gave up. I grew used to it, grew to like it the way it was, angle and all. What did it matter? I was dealing with time, that's all.

14.

Timelessness up there was calendared by the sun, the moon and periodic visits from U Bart. The local people from the village in the valley farmed the terraces below the house. I'd watch them as I worked on the garden. Every week or two, U Bart, a young fellow, a year or two younger than me, drove a donkey laden with fresh vegetables up to our kitchen. He was always smiling; everything seemed to him to be a big joke. He knew none of us at the house talked but it didn't stop him shouting out greetings whenever he arrived. He'd ask after your health as he passed you on the path knowing he wasn't going to get a reply. He didn't care.

Sometimes he'd engage in quite long rhetorical conversation. After delivering the vegetables, he'd mount the donkey and ride it over to the garden where I'd be working, he'd smile and wave and I'd ignore him completely. He'd follow me as I moved around. I'd take no notice. He'd watch me very closely, absent-mindedly scratching the rump of the donkey. The first time he talked to me he was difficult to understand. His English wasn't very good, army English maybe. My conversational English wasn't that good either.

"You not like things way they are."

For a simple countryman he was very astute. He got the point right away. I ignored him and moved on. He followed, scratching the donkey, smiling.

"I U Bart. Name U Bart. "

He pointed to double chevrons on the sleeves of his old, stained Royal Air Force tunic.

"Corp'l U Bart if you like. "

He wore that tunic all the time most of the years I knew

him, wore it with a certain pride as if it was still a symbol of authority.

"I driver for Wingcommandah in war. You know war? You Jap wallah. You fight in war? Maybe we fight each other?"

He laughed. I didn't say a word, just kept on with the raking. He went on his way chuckling, he was a good-natured fellow. It went on like that for two or three years.

15.

It all started one morning late in the summer of 1949 with what looked to me like a forest fire. I'd been living at the house for four years. That morning I'd got up depressed. I'd slept badly. I had breakfast by myself, the first unusual thing of the day. Where was everyone?

As I left the house to go to work on the garden, I saw them, the silent ones. Perhaps I should call them monks; maybe they were, I don't know. Anyway, there they stood shielding their eyes from the early morning sun, staring with more than usual interest to the east. Far away, from behind a distant mountain, a huge column of white smoke was rising, smoke so dense it was beginning to block out the sun. The light diminished, the air grew chill. The monks stood still, expressionless as statues. A few minutes later the sun's arc brought it clear of the smoke, warmth and light were restored. The smoke hung there in the sky for almost a week. It looked like a forest fire, a big one.

When I say that's when it all started, that's when events, concerns from the outside world, began intruding on my peace of mind. I'd been calm for more than four years but the fire put paid to that. Even the monks found it more interesting than breakfast. I could feel anxiety worming its way back into my consciousness. A few days later it took on tangible form.

It was a U Bart day. He'd delivered the vegetables and was crossing the bridge on his way home. As usual, he steered his donkey across to the garden where I was working but before he had a chance to get started on his usual nonsense, both our attentions were distracted by sounds of commotion rising from the valley, a hubbub of voices, men, women, children.

Making its way slowly up the terraces, a motley band of raggedly uniformed and armed soldiers with their women and children camp followers, all loaded down with baggage, all looking the worse for wear, many wearing bloody bandages, some walking, some on litters, a sad sight, particularly the women and children. My mind flashed back to the war, Tokyo, hiding from the bombs in that air-raid shelter. Who were these people? What did they want from us? Food perhaps? Medical supplies?

As they got closer I recognised their uniforms. They were Chinese. Nationalists. Ku Min Tang. We'd fought them in Manchuria. They stopped just below the house the other side of the bridge and collapsed. The women built fires, brewed tea and tended to the wounded while the men sat around and smoked. The children played soldiers. Children make games out of anything and war's a favourite. A young officer who seemed to be in charge climbed up to the gateway.

Suddenly a monk was there to intercept him. I mean suddenly! In the twinkling of an eye! It surprised me as much as it did the young officer. I glanced across at U Bart. He didn't seem to have noticed anything unusual; perhaps he wasn't looking at that moment. It happened to me several times while I was there, out of the corner of my eye, an incredibly swift movement. I'd heard of such a thing but never really believed it physically possible for a person to move so fast.

Anyway, there he was, politely greeting the soldier. There was a rapid exchange in a language I didn't understand, probably a dialect of Chinese, but beneath the young officer's heavy accent I could hear continued reference to Harpur. It seemed he was insisting on talking to Harpur and to no one else. The monk was very respectful, bowed politely, turned back across the bridge and into the house.

So Harpur was alive. I'd not set eyes on him since the day of my embarrassing arrival. It wasn't just that the house was so large and rambling it was easy for him to be there without being seen. I'm sure if I'd wanted to, if I'd been curious, I could have laid in wait, hidden around corners or stalked him, but I didn't. Even if I'd known he was still alive I wouldn't have wanted to see him. He'd figured too prominently in that horrendous chapter of my life. I wanted to forget him. In fact I'd hardly given him a thought in four years and now, here he was, very much alive, walking light of foot out of the house to meet with a remnant of the Ku Min Tang, a young officer who'd talk to no one else.

They talked. I still couldn't understand what was going on but one thing was certain, the young man was the harbinger of bad news. The way he kept pointing in the direction of the smoke, traces of it still hanging in the sky, it was something to do with the fire. They didn't talk for long. Harpur was obviously disturbed. He stood there for a moment then swung around and headed back to the house.

The officer scrambled back down to his scruffy contingent and barked out orders. They began packing up their pathetic bits and pieces, pots and pans. They were obeying the orders but weren't happy about it. They picked up their weapons and crutches and started moving miserably back down the terraces, shuffling, limping, women grumbling lugging bundles, children crying. A sad sight, really. U Bart watched them go, scratching away at the donkey's backside. He scratched that donkey's rump like some people scratched their heads when they were thinking.

I edged over to him. The game of hide and seek was coming to an end. If I wanted to know what was going on I was going to have to talk to him. As soon as I was close enough I came straight out with it. What on earth was going on? What'd Harpur said? What'd it got to do with a forest fire?

He turned around grinning from ear to ear. He laughed and laughed. After all these years I'd actually spoken to him. I let him have his fun. I was embarrassed by the sudden need to communicate after being unfriendly for so long. Perhaps I should have taken my time, been more circumspect. But I couldn't wait. The questions had assumed an importance in my mind and immediate explanations were required.

I felt a little stupid as I introduced myself in a more or less formal manner. We bowed and shook hands. He took it all in good part. He bore no grudge, not at all. He found everything amusing. He seemed to think it was the funniest thing that had ever happened to him. Like I said, he was a good-natured fellow. He tried my patience with his chatter but told me what I wanted to know.

It wasn't a forest fire. Harpur owned real estate in Yunnan Province, the most westerly province of China. It had belonged to his family for generations. The border was quite close by. The soldiers had once been part of Chang Kai Chek's army, the Ku Min Tang. Now they were mercenaries paid by Harpur to guard his property from thieving warlords.

Isolated for over four years, I had no idea what had been going on, no idea what changes had occurred in the outside world. U Bart informed me Chang Kai Chek had been driven from the Chinese mainland and Mao Tse Tung's communists were in control of the entire country and were mopping up what remained of the Nationalist army.

I knew little about Mao or his political intentions but U Bart said it was well known he wouldn't tolerate foreign ownership or influence of any kind and had just forcibly repossessed property that had been in Harpur's family for nearly a century. There'd been many thousands of hectares under cultivation. The smoke we'd seen had been the burning of crops. Harpur's soldiers had been attacked and overwhelmed. They'd been massacred and everything they owned burned, houses, school, hospital, everything. The few survivors that had sought refuge with us were all that remained of an entire regiment. Harpur had sent them down to Thailand to the southeast, to Chang Mai, just across the border. He had friends there. They'd look after them and give them work. U Bart assured me everything was OK.

He was even more cheerful than usual when we parted that morning, happy with our newly consummated friendship. I couldn't entirely share his pleasure. My mind was on other things. I was disturbed by what he'd told me. Everything was OK? The way I'd seen Harpur receive the news, he wasn't happy about it either. He didn't think everything was OK.

16.

I was awakened the following morning by a noise so foreign as to be alarming. In those mountains I had the feeling anything might manifest and this was a demonic monster, slowly threshing and crashing its way towards me, its infernal roaring getting louder and louder, getting louder then, strangely, dissipating into the morning air then reforming, threatening! Then louder than before and closer. I couldn't see anything from the window so I grabbed a knife and crept cautiously outside. There was a chill in the air. Winter was almost upon us.

Like the morning of the fire, the whole household was

out there watching. The noise was deafening. A helicopter was making its way up from the valley, following the terraces. I'd never seen one before. It settled just beyond the gateway to the house creating a great wind that tore at my clothes. Harpur emerged from the house and walked briskly to the aircraft. No waves, no acknowledgement, none of it. He just climbed on board and away they went, back down the valley. What a god-awful noise!

During Kawakami's era I'd paid little attention to Harpur. He'd been no more to me than a cipher, another grey figure in the power game. I hadn't been curious about him at all. Now I wondered about him, making out like a recluse, a monk, a spiritual person existing high above worldly matters when he was really up to his elbows in its shit. I hadn't forgotten what kind of manipulative bastard he was. In little more than four years, he'd transformed America from a self-indulgent, morally weak, isolationist nation into the wealthiest, most powerful empire anyone had ever seen at no small cost to humanity - and myself.

Where had he flown? What he was up to now? My mind juggled permutations and combinations of events, churning out possibilities, building and instantly demolishing monuments of speculation one after the other. I was fired up again. I had to know. I decided I'd go and see him as soon as he returned, come right out with it, ask him what was going on. I had nothing to lose. What could he do to me? My mind was made up. I'd see him as soon as he got back. I had no idea he'd not return for five years.

17.

If you knew ahead of time you'd have to wait five years, it would stretch out in front of you like an eternity. But if you don't know you're waiting, and if you're already operating on the eternity time scale as we were in that remote corner of creation, a day passes quickly. There's plenty to do when you have to do everything yourself.

I'd taken on the cleaning of the house. It was a filthy mess when I arrived; and when the cook suddenly decided not to cook anymore, I took that on too. I organised the kitchen, built storage cupboards and shelves. I cleared the drain and fixed the water pump. I enjoyed doing those kinds of things. I found genuine satisfaction in menial tasks, creating order out of chaos.

Food was no problem. Harpur's family had a long-standing arrangement with the farmers in the valley. They cultivated the terraces and provided the house with all the food it needed, not much, a small percentage of the annual harvest. It was a benign arrangement everyone was happy with.

I fancied myself as a cook. I took over the cooking because I enjoyed it but nevertheless still resented no one else volunteering. When it came right down to it my silent friends were a bunch of idle slobs. When the cook stopped cooking, they all stopped eating, just like that. If they were eating, they weren't doing it in the kitchen. After a day or so, I got hungry, went to the kitchen, fired up the stove and started to cook something. I knew they'd all be back as soon as there was a whiff of food so I made enough for everybody. They arrived as soon as it was prepared and left as soon as they'd eaten, without so much as a nod, like it was their God-given right.

Even in winter when I couldn't work on the garden, couldn't get out much at all, maybe to chop wood occasionally, there was plenty to keep me busy. The winter Harpur flew away in the helicopter I had plenty to think about too.

18.

Spring. It's been described so many times. Even so, I have to tell you that every spring I spent in that valley was astounding. Winter was very set, predictable. It snowed and that was that, the landscape became suddenly transformed. A storm now and then but in the main that's the way it stayed for five months, a white, cold, unchanging beauty - until the spring. The slow warming and melting, the unfolding of everything, the first flush of colour, the flowers, all happening so slowly before my eyes, the growing, the opening.

The spring following Harpur's departure, I took my first hike down the mountain. I'd broken silence with U Bart but still shy of meeting people I'd skirt villages when I came to them. U Bart kept inviting me to his home to meet his family. I was polite about it but always declined. I didn't yet feel ready for ordinary people, mothers, fathers, brothers, sisters.

Later that year, in the summer, I was out walking, following the river down the valley. I paused for a cooling swim in one of its crystal clear rock pools. U Bart saw me first. He was with a ten-year-old boy. They'd been fishing lower down, caught some trout and were going home to grill it, enough for everyone, he insisted. I was hungry and hadn't tasted trout for a long time.

I discovered U Bart to be Headman of his village. He'd come back from the war a local hero. Very few people left the valley and if they did, they rarely returned. Someone who'd left, seen the world and returned had a distinct social edge. Even though he'd inherited his rank from his father, it was fitting he was Headman. He had 'the gen', as he called it. He had the knowledge. He'd seen the world, he could speak 'lish, he could drive a jeep.

He and his family lived in the centre of the village, a quite widely spaced group of ten or a dozen structures housing about a hundred souls. The houses stood on stilts, four or five feet above the ground, elegant constructions with neatly thatched roofs. The interiors were cool and dark, wooden floors gleamed, polished by generations of bare feet. Hogs, chickens and children chased beneath them.

U Bart was married. His wife, Myiang, was very attractive, good looking in fact, neatly dressed and knew all about grilling trout. It's not very difficult but some people do it better than others. The little boy fishing with him was his son and there were three daughters. Asleep on a day bed in the corner was his father, Dran Gu. He was very old. I figured he must know a thing or two about Harpur and must have seen all the comings and goings in the valley. Unfortunately I didn't get a chance to question him on that occasion; he wasn't well and slept most of the time.

They were an entirely modest family. They behaved just like Japanese mountain folk. I felt comfortable with them. I was glad I'd come. U Bart was a charming host, not in the least solicitous. Not a bit of it. Here he was Headman.

19.

It was probably two, maybe three years before I got a chance to talk to Dran Gu; U Bart had invited me to visit for the day. It was some Bön religious festival or other not unlike a Shinto festival. The house was decorated with flowers; everyone wore their best clothes; a pleasant family party. Dran Gu still unwell, slept through most of it.

After we'd eaten, U Bart pulled out an unopened bottle of Johnny Walker Red Label. I couldn't believe it. At the end of the war, his commanding officer, the one he used to drive for, gave him this bottle as a farewell present. He'd saved it, he said, for a special occasion and thought this was it. As soon as the glasses started clinking, the old man woke up. Very soon the three of us were feeling fine. I'd never seen the old man look better. The scotch perked him right up.

As I'd been hoping, when we'd relaxed and settled back, he got quite talkative, wanted to know who I was and then wanted to tell me his life story. It wasn't difficult to steer him onto Harpur. Not at all. He was delighted. Harpur was the major event in his life and he wanted to tell me everything, the minutest details, you couldn't stop him.

U Bart got embarrassed for me and tried to shut him up thinking his father might be boring me with his old stories. Fortunately the old man was irrepressible. What he had to say was not gossip or hearsay, this was first hand information straight from the horse's mouth, an old horse, I grant you. Dran Gu'd been a child when Harpur's father, William Harpur Number One, had arrived in the valley. It was in the reign of the Queen Empress Victoria, he couldn't be more precise than that, William Harpur Number One arrived and decided to stay.

A Tibetan master-builder imported from Lhasa had planned Harpur's house. The men of the village had done the work... that was when Dran Gu's father had been Headman... he'd organised them. Dran Gu recalled the struggle to get the building materials up there, wheezed and groaned as if he, himself, had been dragging great timbers and chunks of hewn stone; actually he was only a small boy at the time.

As soon as the house was finished, William Harpur went away again and was gone for a year or two. When he returned he brought a wife with him. Dran Gu had the idea she was related to the Queen Empress, or at least a lady of nobility. The villagers were happy with the master's choice of wife. The women were concerned she wasn't pregnant but they fixed it. Dran Gu nodded and clucked a bit. They have their ways, those women. Sure enough, she gave birth to a son. Dran Gu's mother had been the midwife. She had birthed the present master of the valley.

Then the strangest tale you've ever heard. U Bart, mellowed by the whisky, started showing a livelier interest in his father's old stories, stories he must have heard a thousand times before. He said his dad should tell me the one about the three horsemen.

Surprisingly, the old man was reticent. He didn't think it was such a good idea. They argued about it a bit but as much as he liked telling his stories, he didn't want to tell the one about the three horsemen, he didn't think I'd like it, he didn't think I'd understand. He'd suddenly grown shy. We all had another drink and by the time we'd finished the bottle he'd already begun.

Dran Gu's father drove donkey-loads of vegetables up to the house, periodically, just as U Bart did. As soon as he was old enough, Dran Gu accompanied his father on these trips, once a week, once every other week. They were occasions for great excitement... he looked forward to them. The cook, when they'd unloaded the vegetables, always gave them tea and sandwiches.

On one of these trips, he and his dad had delivered the vegetables to the kitchen and were sitting outside the house in the warm sunshine, drinking tea and eating their sandwiches. Dran Gu said he was the first to spot them... three horsemen making their way steadily up the terraces towards the house. The Harpurs, with their infant son... the boy was about three then... were taking their tea on the veranda, up on the second storey of the house... anyway, they were taking their tea.

Mrs Harpur had been watching the horsemen from the window. She watched them tether their horses at the gateway, then leaned out the window and called down to Dran Gu's father asking him to invite the travellers to join them for tea. He did. He brought them into the house, showed them up to the veranda then came back downstairs to finish his sandwiches.

A few minutes later Mrs Harpur popped her head out of the window again. She was having a very interesting conversation with the visitors but wasn't sure if she had the right end of the stick. Would dad be so kind as to come up stairs again and translate for her. And he did, and Dran Gu went with him.

Mrs Harpur had asked her guests where they were bound for. They'd told her they were monks from an abbey some five or six weeks ride from the valley, across the Tibetan border. They were wandering these mountains - this is what she felt certain she was misunderstanding - looking for their recently deceased Abbot. Before he died, their master said they should look for him, or rather his next incarnation, around here somewhere. Dran Gu's dad reassured her she'd understood correctly. She was amazed, Will Harpur too, completely intrigued by such strange local beliefs. She asked them how would they know, how would they identify their master in his new form. They smiled at each other. They would show her.

One of them went out to the horses and returned with a cloth shoulder bag. He turned the contents out onto the floor. There was some clothing, one or two books, written texts, a bunch of amber prayer beads, rings, necklaces, a pair of spectacles, all manner of odds and ends. The point to all this was that a few of these things had been very personal to their master in his previous life and he'd undoubtedly recognise them when he saw them again.

While they were talking, the infant Harpur was busy examining the curious pile of junk, what three year old wouldn't? He'd crawled into a voluminous woollen shirt and was trying unsuccessfully to get a large turquoise and silver ring to stay on one of his tiny fingers.

Mrs Harpur scolded him for being impolite, playing with

other peoples toys without their permission. He was told to behave himself. Parents were strict in those days. She insisted he give the ring back to the monks immediately. But he wouldn't. He kicked up a terrible fuss. The visitors were embarrassed. The ring was obviously valuable to them and they tried to get the boy to give it up in exchange for some other gewgaw. But he wasn't having any of it. Wouldn't let go. Screamed blue murder. So they let him hang on to it and he quietened down. Everybody quietened down. No one said a word. Of all the stuff they'd tipped out onto the floor, the ring and the shirt were the only things that had belonged to their master.

After the disbelief came excitement. One of the monks pulled out charts and did complicated astrological calculations all of which confirmed that the child, fair haired and blue of eye like a malamute, William Harpur II, was the true incarnation of the Venerable Rinpoche Ten Sing, thirteenth Tulku in the Rap San lineage, their beloved master and Abbot of the great Chogÿl Monastery in Tibet.

I understood why Dran Gu had been shy of telling the story. He didn't think I'd believe it. But I'm Buddhist. Certainly I believed it. Reincarnation's no problem for me. Even Christianity is littered with those kinds of phenomena. I had no problem believing him.... but I was still flabbergasted, you can imagine. I didn't show it, didn't want him to think I doubted him, didn't want him to clam up. What made my head spin was trying to relate his story to the man who's house I lived in, the man I'd tried to kill, the friend and confidant of presidents.

Dran Gu was tired and wanted to lay down. He'd go on but needed to rest his old back. He wanted a smoke. U Bart brought him his pipe. While he prepared it he continued with the story. Harpur had been delighted. He had no difficulty recognising his son as someone special, someone touched by destiny. He'd been proud. But his wife was less sure. The child had to return to Tibet with the monks to be instated as Abbot of the monastery under the tutelage of a regent, that's the way it was done traditionally. The Harpurs travelled with them to make sure everything was in order. It had been hard for Mrs Harpur to part with the boy but she was a woman of strong character and determined not to stand in his way. About twenty years later... the old man was hazy about dates... the young Harpur returned. His parents had died in a flying accident, locally, not far from the house. He came back to bury them and to take over his father's business.

Dran Gu lit his pipe and exhaled volumes of white smoke. Coughing and spluttering, he offered it to me. I declined. It had a sweet smell, whatever it was he was smoking, not at all objectionable, not like Kawakami's dreadful cigarettes. I asked him what old man Harpur's business was. Dran Gu raised his pipe... let out a lung-full of smoke...

"Opium."

20.

Life went on as normal but I found myself thinking about nothing but Harpur. I still went to the garden every day - it had progressed considerably. I'd smashed boulders to stones, and now a sea of stones surrounded the rock. It looked very dramatic... like one of the islands off Japan's north coast. I still cooked every day and cleaned up a little but Harpur was all I thought about and the more I thought about him the more confused I became. I found myself thinking of him as two quite different people, one secular, the other spiritual, one good, the other evil. All the information about him was contradictory.

On the one hand he was supposed to be a reincarnate being, twenty years the Abbot of some important Tibetan monastery... that somehow fitted with the house, the monks, the way of life there. On the other hand, there was the man I'd met in Washington with Kawakami, the ruthless power broker, *confidant* of generals and presidents and now, opium warlord.

There was little doubt in my mind Harpur's crops burned by the Communist troops in Yunnan were opium poppies. It made sense. The Communists had always made a fuss about opium. "Scourge of the nation", they called it, "A western imperialist monkey on the backs of the people". They had absolutely no time for it and swore to eradicate it. That's what happened in Yunnan Province, no doubt about it. They eradicated some of Harpur's poppies.

He returned in the summer of 1954 but getting to see him wasn't easy. There were no secretaries with an appointment book; he had no prepared schedule to fit into. It was a question of biding my time. There'd be a right moment. I learned that there. There was always a right moment for everything. The right moment would arrive and I'd recognise it.

I saw him on one or two occasions that summer. In winter everyone kept to themselves but in summer they became more visible and wandered around enjoying the warm weather. The evenings could be particularly magical. Sometimes someone would spontaneously perform, Tai Chi, a dance or a feat of magic. One or two of the monks were masters of controlled movement. Harpur was out there once or twice looking on with the rest but I registered no recognisable feeling, no impulse to approach him.

It was the following winter. I was pursuing my self-imposed cleaning duties and floor polishing had brought me to Harpur's door. With my nose so close to the floor it was impossible not to catch a whiff of something coming from under the door, a pleasing fragrance. At first I thought it was incense, until I recognised it. U Bart's house, Dran Gu's pipe. As I said, when the right moment comes there's no doubting it. I stood up, left my cleaning materials exactly where they were and knocked on the door. I could hear him coughing. I waited; heard him coming to the door. It opened.

My old grandfather used to tell me stories when I was a lad, Samurai stories of great battles, feats of bravery and martial skill. He once told me,

"When you do battle with another man, first look well into his eyes. If you see there that he doesn't care, a wise man will put up his sword and walk away."

As Harpur stood framed in the doorway I looked well into his eyes, pale blue, fathomless depths, not staring yet unwavering. I'm sure my grandfather would have agreed Harpur didn't care. But I didn't put up my sword. I didn't walk away. Maybe I was unwise, maybe I didn't care either. He stood aside for me.

I'd been living in the house for nearly ten years and knew it as an austere, monkish sort of place. Except for the kitchen's wooden tables and benches it was devoid of any kind of furnishing. That's why walking into Harpur's room was such a shock. I'd had no idea what to expect. The sudden change took me by surprise.

The place was like a junk shop and just about as filthy. Dust everywhere. It probably hadn't been touched since his father died. Eighteen and nineteenth century European furniture jumbled up with rattan, Chinese ceramics, Persian and Afghan carpets, elephant's tusks, walls of books, paintings, hunting guns, screens, hangings, a large roll-top desk from which, perhaps, his father had conducted his business, and photographs everywhere.

Smiling, he knew exactly what was going through my mind. He'd learned a thing or two about human behaviour, twenty years the abbot of a monastery. Anyway, it opened the conversation. He told me the whole house used to be furnished when his mother and father had been alive. The room we were in used to be his father's study, his library. When they'd died he'd cleared the rest of the house, given the stuff away, family heirlooms, the lot, scattered all over Burma. But he'd kept this room the way he'd found it, the way his father had left it. Moved in without changing a thing.

I walked around looking at painted portraits and photographs. There were scores of photographs. Harpur retired to an armchair, his favourite, next to an elegant eighteenth century coffee table. He picked up a pipe like the one Dran Gu smoked and busied himself preparing it.

He looked different. Fifteen years had wrought changes. I remember how impressed I'd been when I'd first met him, his posture, his graceful, balanced walk, the youthfulness of his skin. He looked much older now but maybe it was the light. He looked greyer than I remembered, dustier, like the room. He lit his pipe, inhaled and exhaled volumes of the white aromatic smoke.

I never tried it. I don't know what are the effects on the central nervous system of smoking opium. I'd seen pictures of opium dens, men lying in tiers, stacked away on shelves. They looked like poor people with miserable lives that opium let them forget, let them dream that things weren't really as bad as they were, let them dream, perhaps, that things were just fine. Who can blame them?

Harpur didn't nod off into a dream, not at all. If anything, the opium seemed to make him talkative, relaxed but talkative. He knew why I was there. He'd seen a curious man before. He knew I wasn't there to talk about the weather or complain about the food. So when he started telling me the history of his family without me having so much as to open my mouth, I wasn't in the least surprised. No beating around the bush, straight to the point without me having to say a word. I sat down in an armchair the other side of the coffee table, got myself comfortable and listened.

21.

A large, heavily framed portrait of a man in his later years dominated the room. A ruddy, whiskered face with bright blue eyes looking down into the room with an expression of benign amusement. It was Harpur's father. He hadn't known him all that well.

A bit of an odd ball by all accounts, born in Virginia in the eighteen forties, one of six children of hard working tobacco farmers. As soon as they were old enough, the sons joined their father in the plantation. Harpur's father, Will, the third brother, turned out to be as green thumbed as they come. Plants responded to him in an extraordinary way. He talked to them and at night he'd wander the plantation playing to them on his flute and they'd grow bigger for him.

The rest of the family thought he was a bit cracked, what they called 'natural'. But they couldn't deny the results; the Harpur plantation produced the biggest crop in the county, the best prices at auction. Will was like a local oracle. Farmers came from far and wide for his advice. When he talked about tobacco everyone listened but if he expressed his opinion about anything else, like frying an egg or politics, they'd humour him and giggle behind their hands. They near split their sides when he said he foresaw war with the North and the destruction of the economy and social structure of the South and that he was for selling up and getting out while the getting was good.

Fearing for their profits, the family tried all ways to make him see reason but finally had to let him go. He'd be missed for sure but a man must be free to follow his own nose, lay his own bets. His father paid him out, gave him his inheritance, as it were, gave him his blessing and wished him well. Will set sail for Liverpool, England, with letters of credit on some bank or other, enough capital to get something going, a farm, maybe a business; he didn't know. On his arrival the bank introduced him to a broker.

Manchester was where everything was happening. Rich opportunities for investment. Trade with the Far East. Cheap raw materials, silk, cotton, tin, rubber, oil, tea, coffee, spices, he was offered participation in a hundred different schemes, the broker calling on him every day with more suggestions. Nothing appealed to him until he met Alexander Dunsmuir, a Scottish Lord. The broker introduced them at the Royal Exchange.

Dunsmuir had headed a powerful consortium of merchant bankers. They'd set up to compete in general trading in the Far East but soon discovered the extraordinary profitability of one commodity in particular. For twenty years they'd dropped practically everything else; they'd made a fortune that most men only dream of, buying opium in India and selling it in China.

But the bottom had fallen out of it. The Hindus were squeamish about the sources of their revenues, got very moralistic about the whole affair and finally managed to persuade Whitehall to impose a ban on the trade and that was that, the consortium had fallen apart.

Dunsmuir was convinced there was another way of going about it. He didn't need the Indians, didn't need the banks either. He needed a farmer, a green thumbed farmer, someone who would scout the continent, even the planet! to find the best conditions and grow the best opium poppy the world had ever seen. Will was fascinated.

In those days in England, a farmer from Virginia, a colonial, was a bit of a joke. Dunsmuir was circumspect with Will. He'd been searching for the right partner for a long time. He had to be sure, had a lot riding on it. He invited Will to his home in the highlands north of Edinburgh for a bit of shooting and a chance to get to know one another, then maybe they'd talk business.

Fate cut short his cautious flirtation. Arabella, his eldest and still unmarried daughter, made up his mind for him. She and Will fell in love. That's what really set the seal on things. Dunsmuir was a widower and had a great deal of respect for his daughter's judgement. She'd satisfied him that Will was his man.

22.

Will set sail on his own for India. He spent a year or so in northern Gujerat where he learned all there was to know about cultivation of the opium poppy, the different strains, relative yields, best kind of soil, the right climatic conditions.

When he knew exactly what he was looking for, he left India, trekked northeast to the central Burmese plateau, then even further north into the remote and rolling Shan hills. He walked up and down the entire range, hundreds of miles of it from China to Tibet, finally finding what he was looking for here in this valley. He camped in the village for two years before settling in. He had to put his judgement to the test, had to make sure he had the right location.

He got on well with the local people. They were amiable, enjoyed to work and liked to please. Dran Gu's father organised them. They cleared the land, ploughed, fertilised, sewed the seed he'd brought from India, tended it as it sprouted and grew. He'd brought all kinds of implements and provisions with him and traded them off with the villagers for their labour; even today they have little use for money. The first crop was encouraging, the second exceeded all expectations. He needed to look no further.

He retained an architect from Lhasa, a man who built houses for wealthy landowners. Dran Gu's dad organised the labour and he started building the house. As soon as work on it was well under way, Will returned to Scotland to report his success to his partner and to marry Arabella.

Dunsmuir was delighted with the outcome, several years patient waiting rewarded. He'd chosen the right man, for sure. He was no less pleased with his young partner's plan to marry his daughter and take her back to Burma. It clinched things, secured things nicely.

Harpur recalled his mother more clearly than his dad, her inner strengths, her self-confidence, her intellect, her sense of humour. He remembered how exciting she was to be with, everything an adventure. She'd told him that's what had appealed to her in his father, his capacity for adventure. The day they wed they left for Burma.

By the time they arrived the house had been completed and they moved right in. They'd brought a lot of furnishings with them to make the place comfortable, family stuff, stuff Harpur had given away when they died.

Will extended the area under cultivation, bargained for more land with local Chieftains and village Headmen. Introduced them to profit, an idea that was new to them, they were still bartering. The poppies were easy to grow and, once shown how, women and children could do it, score the pods, bleed them of their sticky white sap. When the sap hardened and turned brown, they could collect it, scraping it off the pods, just a little from each. At the end of the harvest they'd have hundreds of pounds of raw opium, price by weight agreed, everyone happy.

He organised transportation to the sea, a donkey train to carry it south through Siam to Bangkok where Dunsmuir would have his agent waiting. Some of the opium went to Europe for manufacture into medical morphine but most of it went to Hong Kong and Shanghai for much more lucrative sale. Will knew nothing of these arrangements. He was the farmer, Dunsmuir took care of business.

Even though Arabella remained childless for more than ten years, she was a healthy, active woman. She and Will used to trek, sometimes for days, exploring the neighbouring hills and valleys, meeting local folk, learning their languages, their customs. Being childless didn't bother her, it left her free to pursue her many interests. She travelled abroad with Will on his business trips, once, maybe twice a year. England, France, Italy, Germany. On one of their trips to England they met a photographer in the Lake District. She was fascinated by the new medium and became a photographer herself. The photographs around the room were mostly hers.

In Paris they'd met an early flying enthusiast, some Count or other who designed and manufactured his own aircraft and had an airfield outside the city where he taught his customers to fly. They bought one of his machines and, while Will was busy with pharmaceutical manufacturers, the Count taught Arabella to fly. When they returned to Burma, they shipped the machine with them to Rangoon and she flew it up to Lashio but Will wouldn't fly with her.

He did later but he was shy of it at first. He built her a landing strip just below the house.

Her pregnancy caused quite a stir amongst the villagers. By their custom, the Harpurs were elderly to be having their first child and it gave rise to a lot of superstitious talk and speculation. She was tolerant of their nonsense and when her time came she was happy to have them look after her and deliver her baby.

23.

Dusk was closing in. Harpur lit lamps and candles. My eyes wandered around the scores of Arabella's photographs framed in rare woods and silver. They were everywhere. On walls, sitting on desks, tables, cabinets, a visual chronicle of her life with Will. Pictures of her in flying helmet and goggles; her plane in the air and on the ground; pictures of local people, some of U Bart's ancestors no doubt; pictures of the house; pictures of the child.

Harpur cleaned his pipe and prepared it for another smoke. He made no reference to an auspicious birth and, although he said he was educated in Lhasa in a monastery, made no mention of the Venerable Rinpoche Ten Sing, Abbot of Chogÿl. I only had Dran Gu's fading and opiated memory to rely on for that story.

When Dunsmuir died his equity went to the surviving partner. That's the way it had been agreed. Will became the sole owner of their joint enterprises. He went from strength to strength, growing richer and richer. It took little effort. He had a winner. Everybody wanted to get in on the act, everybody wanted to grow poppies for him.

Most of the northern hills, Burma, Siam, Indo China and deep into Yunnan Province, hundreds of thousands of acres were already under cultivation. Hundreds of thousands of hill tribesmen were gaining a livelihood. He'd started an industry, a complete economy. Opium was the most profitable cash crop in South East Asia.

His influence grew with his success, first in the hills amongst Chieftains and Warlords. By the time the opium got to market he had persuasion all the way to the sea. Sometimes in official places when there were obstacles, sometimes in the palaces of Princes and Kings as far afield as Hong Kong and Shanghai. His last business venture, his swan song, was in partnership with a prominent German pharmaceutical company to produce a derivative of morphine, a panacea, a miracle pill to be sold over the counter at the local chemist shop for anything that ails you, a wonder drug they named Heroin.

Harpur was little more than twenty years old when he received word of his parents' deaths. Will had given Arabella a new aeroplane for her birthday, a new design from a Bristol manufacturer. On it's maiden flight she was taking him for a picnic in a neighbouring valley. The plane got caught in a downdraft and crashed not far from the house just over the ridge. He came home to bury them; cremated their remains right where they'd crashed. Bits of the aircraft's wreckage were still there.

I began to get the picture. Will Harpur had created something more than just a successful business. He didn't intend it but he'd actually created a classic, grass-roots political structure, a hierarchy of dependency. Not just a local matter, either. By the time he died his business had him connected to one or two powerful European houses. He had friends in very high places.

He wouldn't have seen it that way, he didn't look at things that way at all. As far as he was concerned he was a simple farmer who'd had the good luck to be growing something everyone wanted. He was an innocent. Politics? Affairs of State? He had no such ambition, none whatsoever. He'd rather spend his time picnicking with his wife in their enchanted Himalayan valley.

His son, William Harpur II, Ten Sing or whatever you'd like to call him was a beast of a different stripe. As soon as he'd seen his father's will he realised the possibilities. He got a perspective on it right away. What old Will Harpur had left him was power.

24.

After twenty years of esoteric Buddhist training, Harpur had arrived at a lucid view of reality. Detached. No sentimental twaddle. Pragmatic about what is real and what is not. He wasn't bogged down by moral considerations. Good and evil had nothing to do with it, two sides of the same coin as far as he was concerned.

He had no sense of altruism, helping people improve their lot in the world or anything like that. His special view saw all things, all situations and conditions, as equal or at least symbiotic. He saw the world in all its inequity as Perfection, everyone brought to his situation in life in some way accountable and accounted for, the notion of Karma. His fascination for power was not for power as a means to any end. Power to him was an end in itself. Power was the supreme art.

To get the hang of things, an understanding of the state of the world to which he'd returned, its values, its aspirations, he enrolled in the best schools the modern world had to offer. First Oxford, then Harvard for a couple of years, then Bonn and, later, Kyoto university. He was like an extraterrestrial observer sucking up information about another species, learning the rules to a new game, always at the back watching everything, seeing without being seen. He made few friends, only courting, in his shy retiring way, those he thought could be of use to him. He wasn't out for a gay social life, he was looking to expand the network of influence he'd inherited from his father.

Business continued to flourish. Although heroin had been a major pharmaceutical success, the moral climate in western countries stifled its legitimate growth and finally outlawed it all together. It's an old story. Their laws didn't destroy it, didn't make it go away but drove it instead into the hands of organised crime. Sales increased and profits soared. The value of morphine base and the opium it was manufactured from went up and up. Legal or not, everyone in the chain of production, distribution and sale of the stuff were happy with the way things turned out.

He said it was in the early twenties he became aware of the first rumblings, saw the first cracks appearing in the tightly structured, inbred western societies, felt their foundations tremble, saw venerable and decadent empires beginning to crumble.

By 1940 a new picture was emerging, particles coalescing in the swim of new uncertainties. He retired to the house to await developments, to watch and wait. He waited to see if the Hitler Mussolini alliance would make a pact with Japan, he'd spoken to Kawakami about it.

25.

Kawakami. His name broke the spell.

It was dark outside. I'd no idea how long I'd been sitting there listening. Harpur pottered around making tea on an old primus stove by the window. He passed me a cup. We sat in silence, sipping. I thought about Kawakami. Harpur watched me over the rim of his cup. I asked how he'd come to know my cousin.

They'd met at a Moral Rearmament conference in Bern. The ambassador got him an invitation. He knew Kawakami was going to be there and sat right next to him. They'd seen eye to eye on a number of things. He was a mover, a man of considerable power and ambition, someone to be taken seriously for sure. Oblique language couldn't hide his intentions; he was obviously fertile soil for the seeds of possibility...

And the President? I wanted to know how he'd been able to influence a President of the United States.

He smiled, said the boot was on the other foot. The President had been his mentor, introduced him to the finer points of the game. He wasn't President then of course.

They'd met at Harvard. They were both members of the Dinner Club. Somehow they'd singled each other out, you know the way it is, some kind of attraction for each other. They found they had a lot in common; the President's maternal grandfather had also been a bit of a rogue; made his fortune as a trader in South East Asia.

Even in those days the President was crazy for power; politics, he called it. It's all the two of them ever talked about. Harpur'd spend summer vacations with him at his family home on the Hudson, got to know the family well. There'd be a lot of people, parties, sailing, tennis. He and the President would take long walks into the New York hills rearranging the world. He knew he was going to be president, made no bones about it.

Harpur said their close friendship had never been the axis of his influence. He'd never made a suggestion that wasn't one hundred percent in the President's interest. That's what made the nineteen forty scenario so perfect. It was as equally attractive to the President as it was to the Baron Kawakami. Why else would they have acted on it? Kawakami blew it. Things might have turned out very differently if he'd behaved himself. Who knows? Harpur smiled across the rim of his cup.

Perhaps I was a bit tired but he was beginning to get under my skin and he knew it; those pale mocking eyes dragging me back into my own history, less happy times, the war, the bombing, the ghosts of my long dead family. I felt the frustration beginning all over again, coming in waves like nausea. I didn't need reminding. I remembered all right; the burning, the suffering, the atom bombs, seventy thousand lives snuffed out like a candle. It meant nothing to him. A deserved punishment, a slap on the wrist for the perfidious Baron had he lived so long, the elimination of two major industrial cities to be entered in the debit column, a temporary business setback.

I kept it to myself. I didn't bring it up with him. What for? I wanted to hear the rest of the story. I wanted to know what he'd been up to since the Communists torched his poppies in Yunnan Province.

The burning of the plantations wasn't exactly a rude awakening. He'd known it was in the cards. He'd watched the polarisation of the world communities into two camps, made use of the momentum sometimes, pushed a bit here and there, changed the course of things a bit but only in a direction they would readily go. He never tried to dam the river or make it run up hill. He took advantage of the laws of change, he worked with them.

Harpur'd regarded the burning of the Yunnan plantations as an expected signal. It warned of a rising tide of communism threatening to engulf the whole of South East Asia and his poppies. It warned of the destruction of the very source of his power. He'd made advances to the Reds over the years, tentative soundings, but they didn't want to know. There was no bargaining with them, no place for him in their scheme of things. So he turned to the beneficiaries of his nineteen forty stratagem where he had friends in high places, in politics, in industry, in the military; the United States of America.

America, totally crazed by its own self-induced nightmare of communist take-over, wives and daughters raped and children's minds enslaved, that sort of thing, destruction of democracy and everything held dear. Harpur was amused at the simplicity, the way things had worked for him. America was enthusiastically anti communist. "Rather dead than Red!" A natural antagonist to the forces threatening to destroy him.

His military industrial friends needed no persuasion. War is good for business. They were already convinced it was in the best interests of the American people, national security, world peace and all, that the American army should be sent in strength to Indo China to combat the insidious spread of communism.

The Chiefs of Staff were openly scornful of the French

and the predicament they'd gotten into. They couldn't wait. They'd put the *commies* in their place; after all, they were just a bunch of slit-eyed gooks. They lobbied the President, himself a conquering General and a likely candidate for war. He was sympathetic. Agreed wholeheartedly in private.

But Congress was still shy of involvement in distant foreign wars and blocked him; couldn't see what the affairs of people so far away could possibly have to do with America, didn't understand the long term ramifications, ordinary folk rarely did. It needed to be explained to them in the simplest terms.

Their old red nightmare, their worst fear, was being realised. Sure it was still a long way off, but it was the red nightmare all right. Why wait for the *commies* to slime their way into your own backyard? Why not fight them in their own country, the further away the better. That's the way the President set it out for them, in the simplest terms. He told them it was like a bunch of dominoes standing alongside each other, push one and they'd all topple, from Indo China all the way to Main Street USA. Couldn't get simpler than that. A child could see it.

Harpur chuckled. Even then, he knew the army, even a large army, wouldn't be sufficient to ensure the safety of his poppies, the containment of communism, which ever way you liked to look at it. The safety of the poppies would be up to the people on the ground with most to lose, people who depended on opium for a living, the farmers, the *montagnards*.

He said he'd spoken to friends in Central Intelligence about it, about rallying and organising the local folk, giving them weapons to defend their homes, their families, their opium, their very way of life against the Communists. He pointed out to them it would be in America's best interests. The CIA was embarrassed at first by the clear logic of investing in the defence of opium production but they could see he was right. It was in their best interest, in everyone's best interest.

26.

It was broad daylight when I awoke. I was bewildered for a moment, couldn't remember where I was, all those portraits and photographs looking at me. I was cold and stiff and had a headache. I looked around for Harpur but he wasn't there.

Outside in the corridor the cleaning materials were where I left them. I took them back to the kitchen and made myself a cup of tea. It was well past noon. I must have been listening to Harpur for about fifteen hours before I'd fallen asleep. I took my tea outside, sat in the warm afternoon sun sipping it. I thought about Dran Gu as a child sitting right where I was sitting, watching three strange horsemen riding up the valley and all that followed; Harpur's amazing career.

I didn't doubt his story. I knew his credentials and nothing he'd told me was implausible. He had those kinds of connections. He had the power to make things happen like that. He also had the power, evidently, to watch events unfold without becoming emotionally involved in the outcome, a power that knew no compassion. Win or lose, he didn't care. Nothing was sacred, nothing profane. In the holy quietude of the Shan hills or in Washington's halls of power, it was all the same to him.

He was without doubt an extraordinary human being.

Everything about him, his birth, his parentage, his education, everything was unusual. Discount the stories of reincarnation if you like, he was undoubtedly a Buddhist scholar and a Master of *Dyana;* he would have experienced the quintessential nothingness of things, if you know what I mean. It was his fascination for power that had drawn him back into the world. He'd seen the possibility, the unique opportunity to be causal, to start something that otherwise wouldn't have happened, to start a chain of cause and effect. But once started, he had no control over it. It became just another thread, another ongoing theme in the vast tapestry of events.

He got something going in 1940, watched the effects of his power with divine indifference, the destruction of empires, the agony of nations, humanity crushed under engines of greed. He wasn't disturbed by the human suffering he'd caused, had no personal stake in it. He'd exercised power for its own sake; it was his art.

But this time he had a lot riding on the outcome. His status in the world outside the valley, his whole game, everything was on the line. No poppies, no power. His need to defend the poppies left him as vulnerable as anyone else to the vagaries of chance. History he'd created was curving back on him like a wave on the flood tide, beginning to crest and threaten.

His story had overpowered me; the immensity of it. It left me feeling helpless again. But the feeling subsided. After a few days it shrank to manageable proportions. Life continued around me as it had the past ten years and the whole episode receded like a dream on waking. I cooked. The monks ate. I worked on my garden. That was my reality. Harpur's story was my dream. It was just a story after all. What did I know, isolated in the remoteness of the Shan hills. I'd no idea what was going on anywhere else. Harpur himself was like a ghost traversing lifetimes. Part of my dream? I didn't know. Up there amongst the mountains it didn't seem to matter.

27.

I didn't talk to Harpur again for nine years. He was there without a doubt. I swept and polished the corridor outside his room five or six times a year. I didn't see him but there was no mistaking his presence.

A lot happened in those years. The garden progressed. I

scrubbed every vestige of soil and organic life from the rock, a splendid piece of black granite that sparkled in certain lights. All of U Bart's daughters married and moved away from the valley to their husbands' villages, Myiang bore him another son and his father, old Dran Gu, passed on.

U Bart started bringing his older boy up to the house as his father had brought him when he was a boy. When they came up with the vegetables I'd make them tea, a doughnut for the boy. Later on, when U Bart left the valley on periodic trips, sometimes as far as Bangkok, the boy would bring them up by himself. He loved my doughnuts.

During those years, U Bart was my only source of news of the world outside the valley. He never offered to tell me what he did on his travels, I presumed it was business for Harpur, but he was wide-eyed and voluble about Bangkok and the strangeness of its delights.

He said there were American soldiers all over the place; the bars were packed with them. He'd had a drink with some of them. Nice guys. There was no point in asking him what he thought was happening. I don't think he had much idea, even less than I, but it was obvious the world of politics and business was creeping ever closer to our remote home. China had occupied Tibet just to the west of us. The world had drawn close around us indeed.

28.

That summer, it must have been 1960, I was visiting U Bart and his family. I climbed to the veranda and was struck by the incongruity of two backpacks sitting by the door, not local rigs. I listened for a moment to the chatter from inside the house, a mix of English and local dialect and a lot of laughter. U Bart spotted me, drew me inside and introduced me to Timothy and Brenda Straddle. I remember having difficulty with the names.

Timothy and Brenda Straddle were American Presbyterian missionaries. They looked at me curiously, smiling all the time. They wore smiles like masks. They could see I wasn't local. They couldn't figure out where I was from and were too polite to ask. They told their story in tandem. He'd start, then she'd pick up on a point and go on, then he'd do the same, smiling all the time. You could see they'd told their story many times.

Both their families had been in missionary service and were in Indonesia when we overran it and spent the rest of the war in prison camps. They'd had a terrible time. Hadn't we all. At the end of the war their parents had returned to America but they had remained and became married.

Their missionary lives had taken them all over South East Asia; they'd grown up there and spoke the languages. For the last six or seven years they'd been living in the northern hills, moving from village to village, spreading their gospel amongst the hill tribes.

Ever since they'd arrived they'd been hearing the same story, in Vietnam, Laos, Thailand, a curious story about a white god, they smiled, a reincarnate being. It seemed to be part of local lore. Had I heard about it? They'd even seen people make special worship to him in their religious rituals praying for his benign will. Everywhere they'd been, the same story. They laughed again.

They'd been telling U Bart before I arrived, they'd recently been posted to a village forty miles to the east of us and, locally, the story had it that the god lived in this valley so they thought they'd trek over here to take a look. Oh! They were curious! Smiling, they asked was there really a reincarnate being living in the valley? U Bart had suggested they ask me about it. U Bart was busy cleaning fish, smiling to himself.

I took the Straddles outside and walked them a little way up stream to a bend from where they could see the house. It shone in the sunlight like some celestial mansion, way up there in the neck of the valley. The Straddles just stared at it open mouthed. If there were a god in the valley he'd certainly live in a house like that!

I told them it was the home of the *Sangha*, a spiritual brotherhood, a closed and silent order. I was a novice. I cooked and cleaned for them. Yes I'd heard the local stories; they shouldn't be taken too seriously. I reminded them how local people, animists, elevated all kinds of things, phenomena, to the rank of god. Anyone who'd simply renounced the world was holy to them. We joked about it as we walked back to U Bart's house but I sensed they were disappointed. I think they were really expecting to meet a god. Maybe they were relieved.

U Bart invited them to stay the night to get some rest before the long walk home in the morning. We all ate dinner together. I listened to the chatter. Christianity,

Buddhism, Communism; the Straddles liked to talk. After dinner, U Bart brought out a bottle of his homemade wine. He'd told me about it but I hadn't yet tried it. It looked more like beer than wine, had a froth to it. It was delicious, warming and relaxing. The Straddles joked about the iniquities of liquor but both took a glass.

We were into the second bottle. Brenda Straddle was snoring quietly in her sleeping bag at the other end of the room, her husband Timothy talked on alone. The wine had got to him; I'm sure there was opium in it. When he spoke he no longer had the energy to smile gratuitously, his guard was down. He talked less of ecumenical matters, the wine allowed his personal anxieties to drift to the surface.

He told me how, six years ago, when they'd first arrived in Laos they'd been solicited by an officer of the US Information Service. He seemed a really decent fellow and praised their fight against godlessness. And who more godless, he pointed out, than the communists, enemy to both Church and State. We should be proud of the work we were doing making converts for Christ against communism.

He'd visited them again a few months later bringing presents, Hershey bars, magazines, a bottle of wine. He said he'd visit them more regularly in future, once a month maybe. He'd like to get to know them better, he'd like to learn something about their work, their flock; folks back home were interested, would really like to know.

A few months later he asked them to file a report each month on their progress, keep him up to date with what's happening while he's away, make a note of any strangers coming to the village, keep an ear to the ground.

"Wait a minute! What's going on here?"

Straddle said he came right out with it. Accused the fellow to his face of using him and his sacred mission. The officer, a young man so open, so honest, understood perfectly how he felt, but these were tricky times for democracy. Communists were infiltrating, godless and anti Christ. The service he was asking of them was completely compatible with their duty to the Church. A strike against communism was a strike for Christ.

They'd agreed to report to him each month. Straddle laughed. He'd become a spy for Jesus. He laughed but he wasn't very happy about it. Things had changed in South East Asia, very slowly but they'd changed. Since the war they'd changed a lot. There were more and more soldiers everywhere, American soldiers; he'd met them in Saigon. The government there was having a lot of trouble, street terrorism, communist rebels. He felt miserable about the whole affair, didn't understand why his country couldn't leave the natives to work things out for themselves.

They themselves'd had trouble. Hostile young men in black pyjamas had been coming to their village, ranting and raving about Marx and Mao, turning the villagers against them. It got quite ugly and they had to leave. Their Bishop had withdrawn them and closed the diocese.

We'd almost finished the second bottle. U Bart was asleep. The evening was drawing to a close. Straddle had still one more confession, something that worried his Christian heart. He looked left and right as if afraid of being overheard to underline the confidentiality of what he was about to tell me.

He leaned forward. He hadn't been able to talk to the Bishop about it, he'd tried to broach the subject but the Bishop had told him it was none of their business, wouldn't talk about it at all, didn't know what was going on, didn't want to know. Straddle was there in the field. He knew exactly what was going on. But the Bishop had told him to mind his own business and that was that.

He leaned even closer, lowered his voice to a whisper. Did I realise opium was at the root of the whole thing? Did I know that Americans, political and military advisers, were recruiting hill tribesmen, arming them, buying and selling opium to raise the money to pay them, to pay for the weapons? It was all covert of course, nothing official, there was no government funding for their operation, Congress knew nothing about it, these operatives had to finance it themselves by buying the tribesmen's opium and reselling it. They were dealing drugs.

He couldn't believe it. Couldn't believe his America was capable of that kind of thing. The poor fellow was in a moral bind. Wherever he looked, things weren't turning out the way he'd been told they would. He was in trouble. Some kind of spiritual catharsis I suppose. When I left he was praying.

I walked home by the light of a full moon. I remember it well, a singular experience. Day or night, the valley was a place of incredible beauty. I glided upstream from rock pool to rock pool, the moon's silver disc bobbing and rippling in the black crystal waters. I climbed the terraces thinking about the different times I'd taken that path, the first time, crazed and half dead, determined to kill Harpur. I thought of that old mule, the one I slept with.

I thought about Timothy Straddle's confession and remembered Harpur's last words to me back in 1954, his last words before I fell asleep on him. Central Intelligence; grass roots infiltration. I crossed the bridge into the house, the celestial mansion. I thought about Harpur's power and energy, a whirlpool sucking in the whole world upon himself, upon all of us.

29.

There were new faces at the house. During 1961 and 1962 our privacy was invaded five times. Three times by high-ranking South Vietnamese officers, once by a senior Thai policeman, once by a civilian, a European. They came in the summer months, the travelling months, each in a helicopter. I'd observe their arrivals from atop my black granite island as I picked and polished.

U Bart knew enough about Harpur's business to be able to identify them for me. The civilian was French, a businessman from Marseilles, the only one to pay any attention to me. He found me curious enough to take a good look at me through binoculars. Each of them seemed disoriented when he arrived. I don't think they expected to find silent monks, a monastery. More likely they'd expected a palace, wealth, opulence. After all, they'd come to talk opium.

I tried as best I could to weave them into what little I knew of Harpur's scheme of things. They were obviously important factors. I asked U Bart but either he didn't know or didn't want to tell me.

In a way, Harpur's scheme of things was unknowable, so many millions of people involved, a living, breathing culture in its own right. Whatever else, it was obviously hierarchical and everyone at every interconnecting level, from the lowliest Mekong Delta pirate to these high-ranking entrepreneurs, recognised Harpur as boss, no doubt about that. He controlled production and sale of opium in the entire range of northern hills. Why else would these self-important people come to him? To usurp him? To assassinate him maybe?

Whatever the reasons for their visits, they didn't do

much for the tranquillity of the house. Each arrival added to a growing sense of disquiet. The monks, my silent barometer of sanity, began to disperse. Over the past three or four years I'd noticed a drop in attendance at mealtimes. It always fluctuated but some of the monks were noticeably absent. It couldn't have been the food. Certainly I was distracted by the comings and goings, a bit preoccupied you might say, but it wasn't that bad. Even so, by the end of summer 1962 less than half the monks were turning up regularly to eat it.

Then Harpur flew off again. He looked old and tired as he sat in the sun waiting for his helicopter. He didn't seem to really want to go. Something must have gone badly wrong for him to need to leave the valley again. When the helicopter arrived, there were only five other than myself out there to see him go. Maybe the rest of the monks were no longer curious, it was difficult to say for sure. I had the feeling they were no longer there. Things were changing right under our noses.

This time he was away less than a year. I watched his return, the helicopter rising up the valley. I never got used to that damned infernal noise shattering the calm air, a wrathful god trumpeting the importance of its own arrival.

Every time I heard it I sensed a worsening of the situation. It was bringing me bad news, letting me know things weren't quite as good as they might have been.

Harpur got out of the machine, walked slowly across the bridge. The lightness had gone from his step, he stooped, his age was upon him. He caught sight of me and grinned as he disappeared into the house.

30.

Winter set in again. U Bart and his son made their last delivery; the journey was out of the question when the valley was under snow and I wouldn't see them again until spring.

Hibernation had become as natural to me as to any other creature in the Himalayan winter. I moved my bed into the kitchen, the only remotely warm place in the house. I'd keep the old Victorian cooking range stoked and burning day and night. We were well stocked with food, beans, lentils, rice, dried fruits and root vegetables from the summer and plenty of grain. I'd do a lot of cooking.

The winter speciality of the house was the soup. U Bart

used to hide two or three bottles of his home made opium wine in the supplies. He'd never say anything; I'd discover one when I went to open a sack of rice, another in the grain. I'd splash some into the soup. The way those monks savoured it! There were no compliments of course. But the gurglings! The noises they made drinking it! You could be sure when soup was on the menu, everyone would turn up for the meal. Even so, soup or no soup, there were only ever five at table, the rest had gone. There was no longer any doubt.

In the growing confusion of possibilities, the encroachment of the world on our tranquil existence, meditation became my only comfort, my remaining link with sanity. During those winter months, cut off from U Bart, it was my only friend and companion. Sweet *samahdi* from whence the river flows not. Meditation had always been for me a quality of action. During those years of quiet and isolation, I developed the technique of sitting meditation. It was difficult at first, but without it I'd have gone completely crazy.

I continued to make the rounds of the house every month or every other month, cleaning, polishing, repairing. Periodically I'd find my nose to the floor outside Harpur's room. The sweet aroma of opium smoke would remind me of his presence, his struggle to stay afloat in the rapidly changing world outside his valley.

He was never far from my thoughts. I wondered if he'd managed to secure his interests. Were the poppies safe? It had been nine years since our meeting. A lot happens in nine years. I was curious to know. It was time to see him again. Why not? What harm could it do? I waited for the opportunity to present itself, I waited for the right moment.

One night I lay in bed, drowsy on the edge of sleep. There was a knock at the door. I remember wondering who on earth it could be and called out to whoever it was to come in. The door opened and Harpur was standing their smiling, a blanket around his shoulders, then I awoke with a start.

I'd been dreaming. I got up and went to the door. There was no one there. It was the middle of the night. I got dressed and made my way through the house to Harpur's room. A light shone under the door. I could smell the familiar aroma of opium. I knocked and entered. He was sitting in the same favoured armchair, a woollen blanket pulled around him against the cold night. He smiled as though he was expecting me.

31.

Decay. That's what I was thinking as I entered his room. Dust of ages and decay. I sat across from him, the same chair I'd sat in at our last meeting, the coffee table between us.

Nothing in the room had changed. A little more dust maybe, that was all. The same paintings looked down on us, the same audience of photographs peered at us from every nook and cranny. The books, the screens, the hangings, nothing had been moved, nothing added. Harpur didn't look too good, huddled in the blanket, an ancient Pharaoh in his burial chamber rediscovered in later time.

If you grow old with a friend day by day you don't notice the changes, the ravages of time. I saw Harpur so rarely and was amazed at the deterioration. His skin had yellowed, maybe it was the light; it sagged under the chin and around the neck. Bony skull shone through thin and faded hair, grinning lips revealed patches of blackened and decaying teeth. It seemed he'd suddenly become old, old as the flimsy lidded eyes, the same blue watery depths I'd looked into nine years before. They were really old. I could see he still didn't care.

As if reading my mind he said it was in the very nature of things for the body to grow old, to wither and die. Some found it disgusting, the slow degeneration, the wrinkling of the skin and the brown flecks of age, once firm flesh become flaccid. Nothing unusual about it and it'll happen to you if you live long enough. He grinned. He found the processes of corruption fascinating whether in the body or in society. Nothing was forever.

His voice was tired, his tempo had slowed, he admitted it. The game had become too strenuous. The power base he'd traditionally dealt with had fractured. It'd become difficult to create cohesive action. It used to be simple, a question of balance you might say. In its new complexity it had become more like a juggling act, exhausting. There were lots of new operators wanting a finger in the pie. Special interest groups with slick ways of representing themselves to government, bribing their way up from the bottom.

Anyway, he'd done what he could to keep things on

course for a while. Now he was going to take it easy, sit back and see what happened. He no longer had the energy to participate, all that remained was the curiosity. He wanted to be around to see the way things turned out, to see the way it would actually happen. That's what kept him going.

He said we were two of a kind both bound by our curiosity. Mine bound me to him just as his bound him to life. I hadn't looked at it that way at all. I thought about it later. Maybe he was right. Maybe I had been staying on at the house waiting to see what happened. Anyway, he'd got things started, there was momentum. He'd watch the rest of the show from his armchair. Vietnam was going to be the stage, perhaps even for his own Armageddon. He smiled.

He said greed, the thrust of colonialism, still shaped events in South Vietnam. Armistice had bought a little time for the last of the French puppets, the ones in power. They were hard at it gleaning the remains of the harvest, filling their Swiss bank accounts. He knew every one of them. If they wanted to get rich they had to deal with him. His opium was the only stable currency in South East Asia.

The industry was thriving, hundreds of thousands more

acres were under cultivation. A corrupt regime was good for business but a fragile structure when it came to withstanding the political pressures of the day. The armistice hadn't magically made the rebels disappear. They were still there, determined as ever to have their country, to rid it of the last vestiges of colonialism. They'd been giving the government troops a hell of a time. Things had gotten out of hand.

He'd just returned from America where the ferocious materialism never ceased to amaze him. The individual ambition for wealth had become genetic. People prayed their children be born with a silver spoon in the mouth. Presidents head the machinery of government but industrialists and merchants shape the destiny of the nation. Their persuasion is considerable. They were Harpur's natural allies in the situation. It was easier to deal with greed than with principles.

The President in all his years in office hadn't managed to convince Congress, hadn't managed to impress them sufficiently with the seriousness and magnitude of the communist threat with his analogy of the toppling of dominoes. They mistrusted the old warrior, didn't want to be lead into another war so far away from home. Besides, things had never been so good. America was prospering beyond everyone's wildest dreams. They wanted to enjoy themselves, have a good time for a change.

Time ran out for the old President. He was tired. Winning a world war and two terms of office had worn him out. The Presidency went to a younger, more vigorous man not a soldier and inclined to a humanitarian view. His election had given rise to a lot of cussing and swearing in military industrial circles. The last thing they needed was a liberal President. They wanted a hawk and they'd been handed a dove.

The young President was energetic enough and busied himself all over the place quite successfully. He could be firm when he wanted, showed promise and was very popular with the people by all accounts. But lobbying and questions in Congress maintained a focus on South East Asia. Phantom hordes, the rising tide of communism, still haunted the White House.

The President pondered, the stock market held its breath. He couldn't sit and do nothing and neither he nor Congress had the belly for a full-blown war. So he settled for sending military aid and a small contingent of advisers to the beleaguered South Vietnamese.

The arrival of his aid and personnel in Saigon merely exacerbated the situation. Rebels redoubled their efforts, fought harder and brought the war from the countryside right into the city streets, the sidewalk cafes. Worse than that, as fast as America supplied the South Vietnamese army, China stepped up supplies to the rebels. Things were underway.

The President shilly-shallied, wouldn't accept the reality of the bind he was in, wouldn't concede to his Generals' advice to continue the escalation and send American boys in there to do the fighting. If anything, he was inclined to call the whole thing off, that's what his public wanted, revert to the first option of non-involvement. But it was too late. He found himself standing in the way of America's inevitable history. He floundered before the gods of military industry and they'd killed him.

The fear of Communism that'd had America crazy ten years ago had seeped from the conscious into the unconscious and found a nice comfortable place there along with some dusty old flags and rusty sabres. It'd become an emotion, as it were. When the word was spoken or the symbol flashed you could be sure of a paranoid reaction, instant fear, a replay of the old nightmare. When it was arranged to assassinate the President, it was arranged for a communist finger to pull the trigger.

Harpur paused, closed his eyes. I doubted he was observing silence for a murdered President. He was tired. I thought perhaps he'd fallen asleep but he sighed and continued with his eyes closed. He talked very slowly.

A communist had killed their President. Splattered his pretty young wife with his blood. America was incensed and the way was clear for more determined, less scrupulous men. They'd given Harpur their assurance that within five years there'd be upwards of half a million American troops and ancillaries committed to the defence of South East Asia. The poppies were safe. He sighed and paused again. I waited for him to continue but this time he'd gone. In a few moments he was snoring gently, evenly.

32.

I returned to my room. Dawn was breaking. I lay on the bed exhausted yet unable to sleep. It couldn't be true! I remember how I tried to convince myself. It's just another story, hearsay. I didn't know what was going on in America or South East Asia or anywhere else. He could tell me anything.

But there was evidence. The Straddles, the Presbyterian missionaries, they'd seen American soldiers in Saigon and knew something was going on. The Vietnamese Generals, they were real enough. I'd seen them with my own eyes. Was it really happening?

I knew Harpur had the power, influence in high places. I suppose I couldn't believe he'd go so far, gambling his own interests against the lives and well being of millions of innocent people. He'd gone over the top like Kawakami at the very end, childishly capricious with the future he wouldn't live long enough to see, wilfully, maliciously sewing seeds of destruction for future generations to reap. Damn him!

I should have killed him when I'd had the chance. Everything had been so clear to me then, crazed and distraught as I was. I cursed myself for being so ineffectual, for bungling. But it wouldn't have made any difference. I can't explain exactly; it had all started so long ago, had momentum even before he was born.

What about the monks? The silent shadows I'd once regarded as some kind of stabilising element, my register of reality? Where'd they gone? Why'd they gone? Maybe their silent departure spoke more clearly than words of Harpur's slide into decrepitude and corruption, playing on the greed of others, nurturing their corruptibility as he nurtured the flamboyant, silken-headed poppies.

And me? What should I do? Stay? Go? What would I do when Harpur eventually died? I could see nothing to stop me living out the rest of my life there. The picture I was piecing together of the world outside, not so far outside by all accounts, wasn't very attractive. It sounded like the insanity I'd turned my back on twenty years before, perhaps even worse. I had no accurate idea.

I wasn't dependant on Harpur; I could take care of myself. Even if the house had been destroyed by an avenging thunderbolt from heaven I could have survived, my needs were small, not even a consideration. I fell asleep on these thoughts, dreamed I was a child again and lost.

33.

I couldn't make up my mind to stay or go. The argument raged for the rest of the winter, drove me crazy. I couldn't do anything about it until the spring so I stopped thinking about it, put it out of my mind. If I were going to leave, one day, maybe I'd just get up and leave. That's how it would be, that's what I told myself.

By the time spring arrived I was calm again. I watched it come upon the valley with rapt attention, savouring every moment, every movement. The stream swollen with thaw, filled the valley with its roaring. Those springs! The energy! The body wanted to run, dance, fall about. I yelled at the mountains as I strode down to visit U Bart. We hadn't seen each other for five months. There was a lot to talk about.

I'd picked flowers on my way, quite a bouquet by the time I got to his house. His wife, Myiang, waved to me from the veranda. I climbed the steps and gave her the flowers. She smiled. She was pleased and thanked me. I've never yet met a woman who wasn't delighted by a gift of flowers. I followed her into the house.

U Bart didn't seem to be around. She poured tea; said U

Bart had gone on a trip. She stood at the mirror, combing her long hair, watching me in the mirror drink the tea. He'd left over a week ago, as soon as the snow had melted. He'd gone to Chang Mai. She didn't know when he'd be back. Chang Mai was a long way. I knew where Chang Mai was, about four hundred miles as the crow flies, two weeks as a man walks. I finished the tea and she offered me some wine. She complained about U Bart being away all the time. She was lonely and I comforted her.

Before I left, we discussed the victuals that were needed for the house. Her son would bring them up in a few days. I said goodbye and started back up the hill. Despite what had happened between Myiang and myself I was saddened U Bart wasn't there. I'd looked forward to a chat, there were a quite few things on my mind I'd have liked to discuss with him. I wondered what he was doing in Chang Mai.

Whenever supplies were due I half expected to see him trudging up the valley behind his old *moke*, with his son maybe. But he didn't come. We didn't meet again for two years. Nothing much happened during that time, the time he was away. Nothing changed at the house, same number of monks. Every month or so when I was engaged in cleaning the house I'd get a whiff of opium from under

Harpur's door. He was still there; he was alive.

34.

U Bart was back. His son brought word of his return and an invitation to visit. It was the middle of summer and I went down to see him the following day. I was delighted.

He'd got a little fatter, rounder in the face. But the most noticeable change was in his clothes. He wasn't wearing his old RAF tunic with the chevrons on the sleeves; he was wearing a suit, a white shirt and necktie. He looked quite smart.

He was pleased to see me. He'd brought presents from Chang Mai, silk dresses for Myiang, a radio for himself and a bottle of Johnny Walker Red Label for me; he recalled how much I'd enjoyed the last one. I opened the bottle, he got the glasses. We started in on it right away.

It was cool in the house. Myiang was preparing food. We sat, U Bart and I, sipping whisky, far away from the screaming and scamper of children, pigs and chickens. We sat in comfortable silence enjoying each other's company. U Bart said he couldn't see the mountains from Chang Mai.

We sat and thought about it.

It was dark before I knew it. We'd drunk half the bottle and dinner was being served. The food revived our spirits. U Bart started chatting about the special duties of the Headman in village life. After each harvest it was his job to see the crop got safely to market. His own village produced about ten and a half pounds of opium a year. It was the Headman's job to arrange for the mule train to pick it up on its way to Chang Mai. He had to handle the money for them, see it got distributed. Somebody had to do it. That's what a headman was for.

In the last few years there'd been an increase in banditry. There'd always been bandits but there were more of them now. They'd been joined by renegade remnants of old Chang Kai Chek's Ku Min Tang. They had their eyes fairly and squarely on the opium. It had become necessary for the villagers to organise against them to protect it until it reached market.

The family traditionally hired each year to transport the stuff to Chang Mai were a pretty rough bunch of muleskinners, a match for any bandits. There was a certain amount of mutual respect there; they were armed and wouldn't take any nonsense. It was no easy task these days, leading a bunch of opium-laden mules across a four hundred miles stretch of open country. The villages had elected U Bart out of all the headmen to be their representative. The old warrior from world war two, could drive, could speak English. He was their natural choice. His job was to safeguard the interest of the village collective, travel with the opium, not letting it out of his sight until money had changed hands. He'd already made several trips.

Security had become very important. Strangers were appearing in Chang Mai, Europeans; he said they were French. They'd been trying to persuade some of the growers to sell directly to them instead of going through time-established channels. They offered more money for the pound, more money for everybody and a bit besides. U Bart had already made a tidy profit. He raised his glass and we drank to it.

A big highway had been constructed up from Bangkok to Chang Mai; it would be finished next year. He'd thought about taking the opium down to Bangkok himself, direct to the morphine factories where it all ended up. It would be easy, he'd make much more money selling direct, he was going to look into it, knew a few people down there.

He pulled out his radio and switched it on. I hadn't heard a radio since the end of the war, that terrible day on the Rangoon airfield. I took a look at it; made in Japan. He said these days everything was made in Japan, motorbikes, cars, cameras, everything. I felt Kawakami's ghost haunting me. I was very drunk. U Bart twiddled the knobs on the radio until he got some sounds. The signal wasn't very strong, pulsated a bit in the ether, some kind of dance music. He wanted to get up and show me the steps but couldn't make it, he was too far-gone and the bottle was empty.

We parted company early next morning. He walked with me part of the way. He said he'd stay for the harvest then he was off again to Chang Mai, he'd come and see me before he left, come up one day with his son. We shook hands. He looked at me, I looked at him, you know the way it can be with old friends. He didn't come up that summer. I didn't see him again until 1969; he was away over three years. I knew, he knew I knew, things were crowding in on him. Long term arrangements, appointments, everything was subject to sudden change; perfectly understandable. He was off and running, drawn on by his own inevitable history. Aren't we all?

That winter I made up my mind. I decided to go. I didn't

do anything more about it, didn't make any plans, nothing like that, I simply made the decision. I left it to my own inevitable history to tell me when.

35.

Of all the years I spent up there in that house, those last three were the most carefree. I'd decided I was going to leave and felt light, like a prisoner nearing the end of a long term. I let things go a little, didn't take anything quite so seriously. I stopped scrubbing that damned rock. Lichen grew in the crevices, soft springy stuff the colour of emeralds, each spring a fresh crop, brighter and spongier.

I stopped working on the garden all together. I stopped cleaning the house, let the dust settle. Work no longer brought me to Harpur's door. I didn't know whether he was there or not. I didn't really care. The cooking benefited from my newly relaxed frame of mind; a happy cook is a good cook. I'd been collecting herbs, drying, crushing and blending them. They subtly transformed meals even the soup. But no matter how tasty the cooking, fewer monks were showing up to eat. By 1968 only one remained, the one that had the knack of moving very fast. I told you about him. Why did he stay? I've no idea. Maybe Harpur had special use for his winged heels. Whatever, while I was there he ate well.

It was the spring of that year and just getting warm when I heard the helicopter, that damned noise clattering up the valley, my first thought was Harpur's getting out. Everybody else was, perhaps he was too. Then I saw there was a passenger. He struggled out, an elderly Chinese in a dark business suit and dark felt hat.

The monk was there to meet him. I watched from the garden close by, overheard him introduce himself as Doctor Ku, Mr Harpur was expecting him. He looked over at me, acknowledged me with a slight nod of the head. The monk led him across the bridge into the house. I supposed Harpur had called him in to care for his ailing body.

Once he'd got the hang of things at the house, I saw the doctor quite regularly. He didn't come to breakfast, dinner was his meal. He always carried a book and read while he ate. He'd often go on reading long after he'd finished his food, sometimes he'd read until he nodded off, head resting on book; a peaceful soul.

U Bart's younger son had taken over delivery of

vegetables. He only came once a month, once every six weeks. Everything was winding down. His elder brother no longer had the time to make the trek. He was married by then, had a family of his own to look after and with his father away so much, had to deputise for him, look after the affairs of the village like the Headman he would be one day. Anyway, every time his younger brother came up to the house I'd ask for news of his dad. They'd heard he was well but didn't know when to expect him, didn't know when he'd be back.

Then one day around the middle of summer, there he was. I heard him a mile off cursing his old donkey, the same old moke that'd been making the journey for twenty years. He knew his way around, that old fellow. He'd wander off into a patch of corn and grab quick mouthfuls of juicy shoots before U Bart could put a stick to his backside. They were still some distance, still had two or three terraces to climb. I went to the kitchen to put some scones in the oven and prepare tea.

He was alone, got back a few days ago, thought he'd give his son the day off and give me a surprise. We unloaded the vegetables and four small trout he'd caught on his way up and a bottle of Portuguese wine. We took the tea outside, sat in the warm sunshine sipping tea and munching warm buttered scones. He had a lot to tell me.

He'd put on more weight. His tone of voice had changed. It was a little coarser than I remembered. He was more restless, more anxious perhaps, didn't smile so readily. He'd got a car now and a house on the outskirts of Chang Mai. He was thinking of moving the family down there. The house was also his place of business where the muleskinners dropped off the opium, other mule trains besides. He'd become the entrepreneur between growers and buyers for the whole area.

It wasn't all gravy. The mule train had been ambushed several times; some of them had been wounded. One firefight had left three bandits dead on the trail; they'd had less trouble after that.

The police were becoming more difficult. Old arrangements had been forgotten; there was more money around now and they wanted their share. He'd heard they too were ambushing caravans. No one could be trusted anymore.

The road to Bangkok had been completed. He'd made two runs down there in his new car, made good money, well worth the drive. The Frenchies had been on to him again making all sorts of tempting offers, wanting him to join them. Their chief was a man named Boniface, the European that'd come to the house a few years back, the one from Marseilles that'd checked me out through binoculars. So far he'd been able to stall them; they were very powerful, ruthless. He had to be careful. At the moment they needed him more than he needed them. He had the opium.

A war was raging in Vietnam, hundreds of thousands of American troops fighting for their lives. Things were going badly for them. He'd met them in Bangkok, that's where they went for rest and recreation after a tour of duty. He laughed. Bangkok had become as much of a battlefield as Vietnam, an exciting place, one day he'd show me, fine modern hotels, bars, beautiful young women, one day he'd take me there.

Heroin was the big thing in Bangkok. Everyone used heroin, sniffed it up their noses like snuff or smoked it in hand-rolled cigarettes. He'd tried it, couldn't understand what all the fuss was about. It made him nauseous, made him throw up, made him feel dull and stupid. But it was a booming business amongst the American soldiers; they seemed to like it better than whisky or wine. Some of them bought it in quantity to take back to the war when their leave was up, said there was a good market for it in Saigon. He was going to look into it; he knew a manufacturer.

We spent the whole day together. He didn't really know what the war was about. The soldiers he'd spoken to said it was something to do with preventing the spread of communism. He laughed. He knew that was baloney. Why should a country as wealthy and strong as America worry about communism? It was more likely an excuse for army Generals to get rich. He'd heard some of them spent more time buying and selling opium than they did fighting, using their authority, military transports, flying the stuff to morphine and heroin factories in Bangkok, Hong Kong, as far away as France. They were making fortunes! They were losing the war getting rich! He laughed, slapped me on the back, said I was lucky to be out of it all, far away from such insanity. I was fortunate to be living in the peace and quiet of these mountains.

I cooked up the trout for lunch. The delicious aroma attracted the old doctor and the three of us quickly polished them off, washed them down with U Bart's Portuguese wine; fizzy pink stuff. After lunch U Bart and I sat in the shade, snoozing a little on the wine. He asked me about the old Chinese. I told him he was Harpur's personal physician, Dr Ku. He smiled, shook his head. He'd heard of Dr Ku. He was not a doctor of medicine; he was a doctor of chemistry from Hong Kong. If it was the same man, he'd worked for Harpur all his life; he'd set up the very first heroin factory in Asia. Nothing surprised me any more.

The sun was setting between the mountains, U Bart got ready to leave, didn't want to make the journey in the dark, his old donkey wasn't as sure footed as he used to be. I walked a little of the way with him. We walked across the bridge to the garden, strolled over to the rock. He pulled at a bunch of coarse grass that had grown up at its foot. He stroked the velvety mosses in the crevices. He was getting the picture; he was nobody's fool.

The garden told him everything, told him no matter what he said, however bad it was out there, I was getting ready to leave. He held my hand, didn't shake it, held it for some moments, gripping it firmly. He said there were great dangers for me outside the valley then he laughed. What's a little danger between friends?

He said if I wanted to leave he would help me. The best

time would be after harvest, when the opium had been collected. When it was ready for market, we would go together with the mule train to Chang Mai. If we got there safely we'd have a good time. He laughed, he was beginning to relish the idea He'd send word with his son. I thanked him. We said goodbye. I watched him and the donkey until they dropped out of sight beyond the second terrace. I returned to the house satisfied.

36.

Harvest time came and went. U Bart's lad brought the message, a neatly written note from his father. I was to be at his house in exactly seven days no later than sunset. There were no further arrangements to be made, no packing, nothing like that. I had no possessions, nothing but the clothes I stood up in. I continued my daily routine, not allowing my expectations too much rein. All plans are subject to sudden change.

The day arrived feeling just like any other. I decided to leave around noon, the warmest part of the day, plenty of time to get to U Bart's before sunset. The mornings and evenings had already been growing cold; there'd been a few flurries of snow. I went to the kitchen and brewed some tea, put some bread in the oven, ate my last breakfast there alone.

The realisation that I was actually leaving was dawning on me. I cleaned up the kitchen, wandered out into the courtyard, looked around at the house for the last time. I got as far as the bridge then had a nagging feeling I'd forgotten something, hadn't put the lid on something, perhaps you know the feeling; something was drawing me back to the house.

I'd thought not to bother Harpur with my departure. What for? Just to say goodbye Will, nice knowing you? I'd cut through the cord that'd bound me to him and I wasn't curious about him any more. I couldn't care less about him yet, once again, I found myself at his door knocking to come in.

The sweet aroma of opium had been replaced by the stink of chemicals. The room smelled like a hospital, ether and formaldehyde. Dr Ku was preparing one of Harpur's arms for an injection, wrapping a rubber bandage around the skinny upper part of it.

Harpur had shrunk, lost all his body weight, become

wizened, a pathetic ancient creature. He beckoned me to come closer. I sat down opposite him, my usual chair. He looked at me slyly. The inside of his arm was badly scarred, covered in needle marks. He offered it to Dr Ku's hypodermic. When the chemical hit his nervous system he slumped, chin on chest, eyes closed, mucous dribbling from his nostrils. When he finally spoke it was very slowly, softly.

"A wise prince devises ways by which his citizens will always, under all circumstances, be dependant on him."

It sounded as if he was quoting. Shakespeare maybe? I don't know. He said the Americans were pulling out of South East Asia; in a year or two they'd all be gone. He intended giving them something to take home, a token of his appreciation for the trouble they'd gone to on his behalf. He'd set up volume production of high quality, low cost heroin; they deserved the best. He was going to sell it to them on the streets in Bangkok, Saigon, every village, every PX, every foxhole in South East Asia. He was increasing exports to the United States so there'd be a plentiful supply waiting for the boys when they got home.

Harpur had finally gone over the top just as I'd expected

he would. I could see the whole thing, the corruption he'd carefully nurtured and used in others, even in U Bart, it was all coming home to roost, time-honoured order of things was crumbling, Harpur was deliquescing in the ooze of his own putrefaction.

I'd had enough. I got up to leave. Then the most amazing thing happened, happened suddenly in a flash. Suddenly everything seemed sharper to the eye, the light brighter. You know that sort of thing? It happened to me a few times when I was a child; suddenly everything seeming to be a long way off.

The walls and ceiling of the room disappeared, disintegrating in roseate light; a nasal bass drone resonated through my nervous system. I wasn't standing in front of Harpur. I was standing in front of the venerable Tulku Rinpoche Ten Sing, thirteenth incarnation in the Lap San lineage enthroned in a blaze of light. In a flash I saw my whole history, my birth, upbringing, the navy, Kawakami, the war, my frustrated revenge, all of it a predetermined path to him. There could have been no avoiding it. It was a moving experience. Tears in my eyes, I knelt before him and kissed his feet. Then it was over, quickly as that. Harpur looked down at me, asked what I was doing on the floor. There was nothing I could say. I got to my feet and left.

37.

I took my time going down the valley; it was a particularly beautiful moment in the year. After harvest the sun-shrivelled stalks of the spent poppies were torched, hills of them, the ashes ploughed back into the earth to fertilise the next year's crop. The aromatic smoke from the fires clung to the damp mountainsides sometimes for days. I wandered a little.

I'd said goodbye to the house, the garden, the obstinate rock. At the bend in the stream just before U Bart's house I said goodbye to the mountain peaks that would soon be out of sight. I was feeling good, very good, like a child on his way to a party. I arrived at sunset.

***

I'd never known U Bart in any role other than friend and father of children. I'd not met the anxious entrepreneur before. He welcomed me, said we were in a hurry, handed me a bundle of clothing, a shirt, sweater, pants, jacket, socks and boots that laced up. They felt strange on my body, you can imagine. We had to get going.

It was a long walk to the village where we'd meet up with the mule train, shorter by river but we'd have had to pass close to a bandit village so it was safer to travel across country at night. U Bart buckled a belt around his waist over his topcoat and wedged a large black automatic pistol in it. The opium, a burlap package weighing fifteen or twenty pounds, was in a rucksack along with a bottle of whisky and boxes of ammunition. He slung it on his back. We said our farewells to Myiang. There was a sadness in her smile as our hands touched. U Bart slapped the pistol, grinned at me and we were off.

I said goodbye to U Bart's village as it disappeared into the darkness behind us. Later, as we cut south to avoid bandits, I said goodbye to the valley. We walked in silence, he lead the way, knew every step. He'd put on quite a bit more weight and puffed a little.

We must have walked for two or three hours before we reached the next village where we stopped to pick up a mule for me. U Bart had one waiting for him with the caravan a few miles further on. The muleskinners had already been on the road two weeks, riding around the northern hills collecting produce from the villages. They were carrying about three hundred pounds of raw opium when we met up with them.

U Bart went over to talk; I waited at a distance. It was dark, difficult to see what was going on. They talked for a while, turned in my direction once or twice, then they were all laughing. U Bart beckoned to me; everything seemed to be OK. Even allowing for the dark, I'd never seen such a scurvy looking lot, armed to the teeth. As long as they were friends I had nothing to worry about. We all mounted up and were on our way.

Thirteen days later after a hard ride, at about three in the morning we rode into Chang Mai. We'd been riding every night for thirteen nights, light snow and frost all the way. What with the weather and our tough looking bunch of muleskinners, the bandits had kept away, stayed home by the fire I imagine. Anyway, we had an uneventful trip. The whisky had helped. It was raining in Chang Mai and too dark to get much of an impression other than it was a small town. U Bart led us around the perimeter, out into the countryside again, then to his house, through a fenced off division, down a track.

The lights were on. U Bart had a key. He let himself in, came out a few minutes later with a man and woman. They talked in English. They called him Hank. The opium was unloaded and taken into the house. U Bart and the leader of the mule train weighed it, entries were made in a ledger and money changed hands. Then they were off again, the muleskinners, just like that. Did their business and left. They didn't mind the rain.

I woke up the following day late in the afternoon. It was still raining. U Bart had gone out. The young couple were very friendly, putting themselves out to make me comfortable. I think they were Australian. Hank paid them to look after the house when was away. They'd washed and pressed my clothes. I showered and got dressed.

U Bart was in a cheerful mood when he returned just after nightfall. He was filthy with mud and grease; he'd been in the garage playing with his car. As soon as he'd cleaned up, the four of us sat down to an evening meal.

After we'd eaten, the young people retired to their room, U Bart and I sat with a bottle of scotch, music on the radio. He asked what I planned to do now I was back in the world. I'd honestly not given it a thought but didn't hesitate, heard myself say I was going back to Japan. He nodded. Back to Japan. It seemed to make sense to him.

There was something on his mind. He didn't want to alarm me but wanted me to be aware of the situation. The opium business had its dangers. It wasn't just the police, there were people out there who'd kill for the stuff. It was like gold, had high international value, any thief who could get his hands on it sold it straight back into the market. That's what the police did too; you had to be careful. Whether I liked it or not, I was involved, knew people, names, knew more about what was going on than was good for me. I knew what he was talking about. He thought it was a good idea for me to go back to Japan. As much as he would miss an old friend it would be safer for both of us. When we got to Bangkok he'd see if he could help, see if something could be arranged. He still had business to attend to in Chang Mai; we'd leave for Bangkok in a day or two.

The following day, two Europeans drove up to the house, I saw them from the window, two men. I didn't let them see me; I was already paying attention to U Bart's warning. He let them in; they also called him Hank. He took them into the back room where he kept the scales and the opium.

The walls were thin, I couldn't help but hear the visitors' voices raised in excitement, annoyed, not entirely happy about something. U Bart in softer tones, calming them down with reason, apologetic. They left a half hour later carrying two large and heavy suitcases. They were not happy, jabbering at each other in French.

U Bart couldn't stop grinning. As soon as they'd gone he told me he'd sold them a hundred pounds, told them it was all he had, for the best price yet! Such fools! He'd told them it had been a poor harvest, the stuff was scarce and he had to charge more for it. Late spring, early winter, a hundred pounds was all there was. They didn't believe him but there was nothing they could do about it. What did they know about growing poppies? He laughed. He'd sell the other two hundred pounds at much greater profit down in Bangkok direct to the factories.

He had to watch those Frenchmen, had to keep an eye on them. They were still trying to get him to work for them exclusively, offered huge sums of money. He didn't need their money. He'd already got more than ten thousand dollars US saved in the bank. He didn't trust them. If he started working for them they'd move right in, soon they wouldn't need him, then what? He drew a finger across his throat and laughed. As long as they needed him he was safe. We set off for Bangkok the following morning.

38.

I helped him wash the car before we left. It looked very respectable, an English car, not too old and quite comfortable, plastic flowers hung from the driving mirror. He was a good driver; bragged the car could do a hundred. The new highway tempted him to show me but he didn't want to attract attention, we were carrying two hundred pounds of raw opium. I hadn't seen where he'd hidden it. It wasn't in the boot and neither was it in the car with us. It was none of my business where it was.

We didn't talk much; he wasn't in the mood. He was sweating; I could smell his adrenaline. I'd not seen him nervous before. Nothing happened, the journey was without incident, but you have to sweat, you never know. It stopped raining but the countryside remained shrouded in mist. I didn't see much. It was dusk by the time we got to Bangkok.

We drove around. There were new suburbs, boxy structures of painted concrete, neon signs, the new world, the 'battlefield' U Bart had told me about. We headed into this garish and noisy wonderland.

He drew to the curb and stopped, pulled out some folded bank notes and gave them to me. I tucked them away. He said there was a bar around the corner called the *Oasis*. He had to leave the car at the garage, pointed it out across the road; something needed fixing. He'd join me in the bar in about an hour.

What a place! That bar! The *Oasis* or whatever it was called. Crowded with young American soldiers, cigarette smoke, dance music so loud people were shouting their conversations at the tops of their voices. Beautiful young girls in scanty underwear slithered between the clientele serving drinks and collecting glasses. As soon as I found a seat, one of them was on me, sat herself squarely on my lap; a beautiful creature. I was completely charmed. She stroked my face, called me uncle; asked what I wanted to drink. She was only about seventeen. She brought whisky for both of us. I paid her. She asked if I'd like to come upstairs with her; the bar was on the ground floor of a six storey hotel; she had a room. I noted the time. I was back in the bar in less than an hour. U Bart wasn't there. I ordered another drink, waited another hour.

Still no sign of him, I walked back to the garage. The place was deserted. The lights were on at the back. I tapped gently on the front office door. No watchman, nothing. The door was unlocked. I went in. I listened. Nothing. I called out softly. No reply. I went through the office into the work area.

U Bart's car was at the back. It had been stripped, the wheels were off, the seats had been torn out, the bonnet was open, the boot was open. U Bart was dead, sprawled inside the car, two or three bullets in the head, close range by the look of it. There was nothing I could do. I found the light switch, turned out the lights. As I left, I thought about Boniface the Frenchman scrutinising me through binoculars. I walked to a quieter part of town. I needed to be by myself.

39

I found a hotel, a modest looking place; the concierge asked me for my passport. Passport? It had never occurred to me. Passport! Whatever identification I'd had was gone long ago when I turned up at Harpur's house. Lost. Destroyed. Who knows? I told him I'd left it in the car and turned to leave. He said it could wait until morning. I paid for the room in advance; that's all he cared about.

I lay in bed thinking about poor U Bart. His murder had brought the wheel full circle. Corruption had touched the heartland. Sleek and greedy rats had found their way into old Will Harpur's enchanted Himalayan kingdom. It was all over. The poppy lied like a diseased whore, all the evils of the world festered beneath her innocent bloom. I fell into a long deep sleep and didn't wake until noon the following day. The chambermaid was banging on the door wanting to get on with her work.

I took a cab to the Japanese embassy; no one followed me. I told them I'd lost my passport. I was directed to an office where a Vice Consul dealt with such things. He asked if I had any identification at all. I said I'd lost everything. He gave me a form to fill out.

He looked at what I'd written. He was incredulous. I'd

lost my passport somewhere in northern Burma? 1945? Where had I been? What had I been doing for the last twenty-five years? I told him I was on active service in that part of the world when the war ended, no reason to return to Japan, my family had all been killed. I'd entered a local monastery.

He asked me to wait and withdrew to an inner office. I could hear him talking on the telephone. He was back in about ten minutes. The Ambassador would like to interview me.

He was very courteous, the Ambassador. He enquired politely if I was one of the Terumasa of Nagasaki. I was in luck. He'd served with my father during the war. Could you believe it? He'd been a lieutenant on my father's last ship torpedoed off Guam. He recalled my father's gallantry; he would be honoured to be of service to the son.

He needed more information, everything had to be verified officially of course, photographs, finger prints, as much personal family information as I'd be pleased to give. It all had to go to Tokyo. It would take a few days. He gave me a temporary document and some money for which I signed and he arranged a room for me at an hotel where he lodged diplomatic visitors. He promised to call me the moment there was news.

I wasn't paranoid but took precautions. I didn't leave the hotel. I spent the next two or three days in the lounge watching television. I'd never seen a television before and became glued to it. A number of the guests were western newspaper correspondents, Americans, Europeans, a drunken lot in South East Asia to report the Vietnam War. They'd gather around the television to watch news broadcasts two or three times a day. I think some of them reported the war from there.

One day we watched an American General interviewed in the smoking ruins of some ancient city he'd just regained from the rebels, temples and palaces of great beauty that had stood for thousands of years, now piles of rubble beneath his combat boots. He was saying he'd had to destroy the city to save it. The newspapermen cheered and ordered another round of drinks.

The Ambassador called. Everything had been confirmed. It gave him a great deal of pleasure to tell me everything was in order. We agreed to have dinner. He came to the hotel. He told me the Terumasa estate had been incorporated into the city of Nagasaki. Over the years much of it had been sold off to private interests. The castle, our home at Sakuradai, had gone in the bombing.

The minister for home affairs was looking into it; the circumstances were unusual, I'd returned from the dead, as it were. The city had incurred a lot of expense, there wasn't much left that could rightfully be called mine but he'd been assured I'd be well looked after. I couldn't expect to be a power in the land but there'd be enough to keep me comfortable for the rest of my life. We drank to it.

There wasn't enough he could do for me. He offered to advance as much money as I thought I might need and recommended a shipping line, an old fashioned freighter that carried a dozen or so passengers in style; he knew the owners. His secretary would book a passage for me. He was as fine a gentleman as you could wish to meet.

I went back to the hotel. Tried to collect my thoughts. Everything was settled. I could return to Japan with honour and spend the rest of my life in comfort. I'd buy a piece of land in the countryside near where our old ancestral home had stood at Sakuradai, maybe build a small house there, a garden. But something about this plan troubled me, niggled away in a corner of the mind.

.I began to worry there might not be room for me in modern Japan, that I would feel as uncomfortable and out of place there as I had in the past. Not only that, I couldn't shut out thoughts of U Bart's wife, Myiang. No one had told her. She didn't yet know what had happened. What would she do now? How would she sustain herself? Certainly she was still young enough and attractive enough to find another husband. I remembered the way she looked at me in the mirror as she brushed her hair.

The following morning I returned to the embassy. The Ambassador wasn't there, away on some business or other. He'd left instructions with his secretary to give me money and travel documents. She'd made arrangements with the shipping company. I would have to hurry. The ship that would take me back to my homeland sailed at midnight. She wished me a pleasant journey.

I spent the rest of the day doing a little shopping; some clothes, a rucksack to carry them in and a bottle of whisky. It was evening when I walked to the bus terminus and boarded the bus bound for Chang Mai.

.

27421117R00091

Made in the USA
Columbia, SC
27 September 2018